The 50 Best
PIZZAS
in the World

Also by Honey and Larry Zisman

The 47 Best Chocolate Chip Cookies in the World
57 More of the Best Chocolate Chip Cookies in the World
The Great American Peanut Butter Book
The Burger Book
The 50 Best Cheesecakes in the World
The 50 Best Oatmeal Cookies in the World
The 55 Best Brownies in the World
Super Sweets
The Great International Dessert Cookbook
Chocolate Fantasies
The Ultimate Lunchbox Book
Let's Have a Party!

The 50 Best PIZZAS in the World

The Irresistable Winners of the Passion for Pizza Contest

Honey and Larry Zisman

St. Martin's Griffin
New York

Design by James Sinclair

Library of Congress Cataloging-in-Publication Data

Zisman, Honey.
    The 50 best pizzas in the world : the irresistible winners of the passion for pizza contest/Honey and Larry Zisman.—1st St. Martin's Griffin ed.
      p. cm.
    Includes index.
    ISBN 0-312-20632-1
    1. Pizza. I. Zisman, Larry. II. Title.
TX770.P58Z57   1999
641.8'24—dc21   99-23144
                                                          CIP

10 9 8 7 6 5 4

for
Samantha, Sean, Emily, and Corina

May they always enjoy the slices of life

pizza, n. a flat, open-faced pie of Italian origin, consisting of a crust topped with tomato sauce and cheese, often garnished with anchovies, sausage slices, mushrooms, bacon, olives, etc.

—Webster's Encyclopedic Unabridged Dictionary of the English Language

AND THAT'S ONLY THE BEGINNING!

CONTENTS

The 50 Best
PIZZAS
in the World

America's Favorite Food
An Introduction

Name a food that's good for you, quick and easy to make, available just about everywhere, suitable for both meals and snacks, comparatively inexpensive, and very much loved by children. And tastes great and fills you up. You'd have to say "Pizza!"

Pizza has truly become the universal food, served in more restaurants in the United States than any other food. It is available for take-out, it can be delivered hot to your door, it can be found ready-made in the supermarket, and, best of all, it can be made at home.

And like most things, it is best when you make it yourself at home.

You can make the crust the exact thickness or thinness you like, you can bake it exactly to your own desires, and you can choose which toppings and how much of each one you want.

Whether you like a basic pizza with tomato sauce and cheese, a white cheese–only pizza, or exotic combinations of meats, fish, seafood, vegetables, and fruits, you can have it your way when you make it at home.

Because it has been so easy and convenient to pick up a pizza on the way home from work at one of the many, many pizzerias found just about everywhere, call up and order one for delivery, or choose from a large variety at the frozen food case at the supermarket, many people have not pursued the joy and satisfaction of making their own at home.

But now is your chance . . . and whether you are a first-time home pizza baker or an experienced pizza maven, you will create masterpieces with the winning recipes from the national Passion for Pizza recipe contest.

Here is the best of the best, a delightful collection of pizzas for everyone. No matter which recipe you make, no matter which crust you use, no matter which toppings you choose, no matter which sauce you make, you, too, will be a winner because you will be making and eating the very best pizzas in the land.

Pizza: A Great Moment in American History

It is hard to believe that pizza, something so essential to modern life, has not been around since the beginning of time. But in truth, although there were early predecessors that resembled pizza, pizza as we know it has been around only a little more than 100 years which is only like yesterday in the long history of the world.

Ancient breads that contributed to a taste for "pre-pizzas" include the pita breads of the Middle East and the flat, seasoned breads that were eaten from Morocco all the way to India.

Roman legionnaires stationed in Palestine discovered the unleavened bread native to that part of the world and then added herbs and olive oil to make the bread tastier. (Matzoh, therefore, can rightly be considered one of the early ancestors of pizza.)

The soldiers returned to Rome from the Holy Land and brought back with them ideas and foods learned from service in that foreign country. Soon other people in Rome started eating as appetizers and snacks round pieces of bread topped with seasonings and oil. Around the year 1,000 A.D. these tasty round breads became popular in Naples and Neapolitans added the word "picea" to their dialect. It is believed that the word evolved from an old Italian word meaning "to pluck" or "to pinch," describing how the hot pieces of bread were taken out of the ovens.

Besides the importation of different styles of bread from other countries, Pompeiians enjoyed a coarse bread dough formed into a rectangle or circle and topped with olive oil and baked in crude wood-fired ovens.

Although pizza was sold in the streets from open-air stands, its popularity spread even to Italian royalty.

Guests attending receptions given by the Bourbons northeast of Naples at the Palace of Caserta dined on pizza, and King Ferdinand IV had pizza cooked in the Capodimonte ovens when they were not otherwise occupied making porcelain pottery. Marie Antoinette's sister,

Queen Maria Carolina, had ovens built in the forests so she could have pizza when she and her friends were out hunting.

Since tomatoes, one of the main ingredients of the pizza we know and love so well, were native only to the New World, it was a long time before tomatoes were added to the herbs, spices, and toppings on the round breads.

Although some of the first European explorers in the early 1500s brought tomatoes back with them from their trips to what is now South America, it took about 200 years for Europeans to accept the tomato as something they could—and should—eat.

The most adventurous in the use of tomatoes were the poorer people of Naples who started adding tomatoes to their baked round breads. Although more adventurous travelers would visit the deprived sections of Naples to sample the native foods, pizza with tomatoes remained a food for the peasants until 1830.

In that year the world's first pizzeria opened in Naples. It was called Port'Alba and used ovens lined with lava from Mount Vesuvius. The new restaurant quickly became popular with the trend-setters in Naples.

The cheese and tomato sauce pizza of today did not appear on the scene until about 100 years ago. In honor of Queen Margherita, consort to King Umberto I of Italy, Don Raffaele Esposito, owner of the Pietro il Pizzaiolo in Naples, responded to a royal summons for a special dish to honor the Queen. He created what we now consider the traditional pizza as an homage to the Italian flag when he added a new color—the white of mozzarella cheese—to the red tomato and the green basil that had been the usual style of pizza up until then.

From that day on, the tomato, basil, and mozzarella cheese pizza was known as Pizza Margherita—and it still is today.

Italian immigrants brought pizza to America in the later part of the 19th century. The first pizzeria in America—Lombardi's—was started in 1905 by Gennaro Lombardi on Spring Street in the Little Italy section of New York City. (Several years ago Andrew Bellucci re-opened Lombardi's pizzeria in its original building on Spring Street. A cracked oven forced him to move the restaurant across the street, where Lombardi's continues to bake great pizzas.)

For the 40 years following Mr. Lombardi's opening of that first pizzeria, pizza was enjoyed almost exclusively by Italian-Americans within their own neighborhoods.

Happily, that isolation dissolved after World War II.

During the war American soldiers who visited Naples discovered pizza and when they returned home to the United States they wanted to continue eating that wonderful combination of baked bread, sauce, spices, and toppings they had discovered in Italy.

Pizza was now "hot," growing in demand, and a craze for pizza swept America that continues to this day.

While early pizza lovers were satisfied with tomato sauce, cheese, and a very limited selection of toppings, today's aficionados have come to expect an amazing array of variations.

Although the basic pizza is still enjoyed by many, this once simple food has grown into gourmet versions—some would say gourmet excesses—with a variety of grains and styles of crusts, and toppings of duck, sausage, bison meat, clams, Cajun shrimp, kung pao shrimp, spinach, garlic-glazed chicken, cavier, fiddlehead ferns, truffles, wild mushrooms, leeks, smoked salmon, pineapple, goat cheese, feta cheese, spiced pumpkin, sun-dried tomatoes, and honey ham.

While some of the pizzas in the United States today would still be recognizable to Signor Esposito and Signor Lombardi, many others are uniquely modern and uniquely American—so American, in fact, they might well give rise to a new catchphrase: "As American as a pizza pie."

Choosing the Best Pizzas in the World

Picking the 50 best pizzas from thousands of recipes that were received in the national Passion for Pizza contest is no easy task . . . but it is certainly an enjoyable one when you get to taste so many varieties of a favorite food.

With so many delicious choices, how, you might ask, do you select the best?

First, we look for recipes that are a little different, something out of the ordinary, something that sets them apart from all the others. It can be a creative combination of ingredients giving a unique flavor, or the addition of one special spice or garnish that makes for a tasty treat not experienced before.

Some of these special qualities are seen in the lox and cream cheese pizza, which is a new twist on the usual lox and cream cheese combination on a bagel, and in the blue cheese and pear pizza, which is a nice alternative to the usual tomato sauce and cheese.

Or what about artichoke hearts and spinach, a combination that says here is a pizza that is different and delicious?

Second, the ingredients should not be so exotic or rare that home pizza bakers will not be able to find the ingredients to make the winning recipe. It is important to choose winning recipes that call for ingredients that everyone will be able to get regardless of where they live.

And, finally, the winning recipes are neither overly complicated nor difficult to make. What good is a delicious recipe if most people do not have the time or the ability to make it? Therefore, while not looking for recipes that are just simple and easy, every winning entry is one that can be readily prepared by most home pizza makers.

We hope you get as much enjoyment making and eating these great pizzas as we did selecting them. It was a hard job but it was a labor of love . . . and a labor of good eating!

Essential Utensils and Some Good Advice

Tools of the Trade

Making pizza at home does not require any expensive, complicated, computerized, or specialized equipment that comes with an instruction manual 100 pages long and takes hours to learn how to use.

All you really need are three supplies, all of which are readily available at cookware and houseware stores for a total cost of less than $45.00 combined.

The first tool is a pizza stone made of unglazed tiles. The tiles absorb and radiate the heat in a regular home oven, cooking the crust quickly and giving the pizza the slightly charred taste it gets in a wood-fired oven.

Second, you'll need a pizza peel. A peel is a large wooden spatula that is necessary for sliding the pizza onto and off of the pizza stone in the oven. (While home cooks usually opt for a wooden peel, professional chefs often use a heavy-duty metal variety.)

The pizza can be made right on the peel and then put into the oven. After the dough has been rolled out into the shape of the pizza, carefully fold the circle in half and then in half again, picking up the quarter-sized crust and gently placing it on the peel and unfolding it so the crust lies flat. (Before putting the unbaked pizza crust on the peel, it is wise to sprinkle the peel with a generous coating of cornmeal to ensure that the crust does not stick to the peel when you are sliding it onto the pizza stone in the oven.)

After the unbaked crust is placed on the peel, the sauce and toppings are added, and the unbaked pizza is transported to the oven right on the peel.

The third item—a circular rolling wheel pizza cutter—may not be absolutely essential but is certainly nice to have. Although you could get along with using a regular kitchen knife, a circular cutter is much faster and makes cleaner cuts. Equally important, using a circular cutter makes you feel like a real pizza-making maven as you run it back and forth across the pizza creating the perfect wedge-shaped slices.

Some rolling wheel cutters come with a protective blade cover and are made so you can replace the blade. While such extras are nice, they raise the price of the cutter and are not really necessary unless you start turning out hundreds of pizzas a week.

Beyond these three essential utensils, there are several other tools that are also helpful.

Instead of a pizza stone, some pizza bakers prefer using a pizza screen, a flat wire-mesh pan with a solid rim. Since the sticky bottom of an unbaked pizza crust could cause a slight problem when sliding the pizza off the peel onto the pizza stone in the oven, a pizza screen can make the task easier.

The unbaked pizza can be made right on the screen or it can be placed on the screen after the sauce and toppings have been added to the crust. The screen with the unbaked pizza is then put onto the peel for placing in the oven.

The screen should be sprayed with vegetable oil before placing the unbaked crust on it to avoid having the crust stick to the screen. Another use for the screen is that you can bake a pizza in the oven right on a rack in the oven without having a pizza stone.

A spatula in the shape of a pizza wedge—or a large pie server—is useful when serving the slices of a large pizza and you would rather not use your hands, especially if you are giving out pizza slices to visiting friends and relatives.

If you are making deep-dish pizza, it is necessary to have a pizza pan that will hold the pizza together as you make and bake it. Do not bake flat pizzas in a baking pan since they will become greasy and soggy because the sides of the pan trap the oil and moisture and prevent them from escaping during baking.

It is handy to have a good-quality serrated bread knife for cutting deep-dish and stuffed pizzas since the circular cutter will not work well with these thicker pizzas.

A Few Notes on Ingredients

- Whenever possible, use fresh herbs, spices, and vegetables rather than dried or frozen ones. Fresher is always better, giving a fuller flavor, and working with fresh ingredients gives a good feeling.
- Extra-virgin olive oil is the preferred choice, since its bold, distinctive flavor enhances the pizza.
- It is the mozzarella cheese that gives pizza the traditional long strands of melted cheese. If you would rather have a less stringy texture, substitute fontina cheese for some of the mozzarella.
- Keeping in line with the traditional Neapolitan pizza and giving the pizza a more tart flavor, use buffalo milk mozzarella cheese instead of the mozzarella that is usually used.
- There are many low-fat and nonfat versions of cheeses and meats that have the same flavor as the full-fat versions. You can feel confident in using those versions without losing the taste you are used to enjoying.
- If you like your foods spicy and want to make your pizza "hotter," the McCormick company has Spicy Pizza Seasoning—Hot Flavor, a small jar with a label that says "Shake on the flavor! A spicy blend of crushed red chili peppers with the perfect amount of garlic and Italian herbs."

. . . And Some Tips About Technique

- When sautéing garlic for the pizza topping, use low heat and cook only until the garlic becomes soft. Cooking too long makes the garlic extra bitter.
- Dough rises best when the temperature is 75 to 85 degrees F. Allowing the dough to rise in a hotter temperature could harm the yeast.
- Keep in mind that the weather can affect the preparation of the dough when making the crust. The dough will be stickier than usual on hot, humid days. Add small amounts of flour at a time—between a teaspoon and a tablespoon—to decrease the stickiness of the dough.

- Unused pizza dough can be frozen while still in a ball or after it has been rolled out into a circle for the crust. Thaw the frozen dough in the refrigerator over a period of a day or two or for a couple of hours at room temperature.
- Left over pizza slices from lunch or dinner . . . if there are any left over . . . can be frozen to be eaten at another time. Wrap the slices tightly in plastic wrap and then cover with aluminum foil or freezer wrap or place in a sealed plastic food storage bag.
- Although almost all the recipes in this book give instructions for using an oven, for something a little different you can try grilling the pizza on an outdoor gas or charcoal grill. Since cooking temperature varies so much when grilling, it is necessary to keep a close watch on the pizza as it is cooking on the grill. Practice and experience will give you the expertise to make terrific pizzas outdoors.

Pizzas Triumphant:
The 50 Winning Recipes

Pizza is such a popular food—served in so many countries and made in so many homes and created with so many different varieties of crusts, sauces, and toppings—that it was not easy to select the 50 very best pizzas in the world.

Here are the 50 best of the best, chosen from thousands of recipes, every one of them a fine pizza. Whether you're in the mood for traditional Italian fare or something completely new and unexpected, you'll find plenty of reasons to fire up the oven.

Buon appetito!

Crusts:
Foundations for the Perfect Pie

Back in the 1950s Johnnie Ray had a hit song called "Build Your Love on a Strong Foundation" and if you do, according to the song, true love will be yours.

In a similar way, you should build your pizza on a strong foundation—a good tasty crust—and great eating will be yours too.

Since a perfect crust is a creation unto itself, here are seven tasty crust recipes to be used with the winning recipes for sauces and toppings in this book. Each can be mixed and matched with any of the 50 pizzas in the collection.

Basic Crust Number 1 has honey for those people who would rather not use refined sugar and prefer a more natural crust. More honey—another $\frac{1}{2}$ to 1 teaspoon—can be added for a slightly sweeter taste. This crust comes out crispy on the outside and moist on the inside.

Basic Crust Number 2 differs from Basic Crust Number 1 in the use of sugar rather than honey and more olive oil is included. The difference in flavor between using honey and sugar is very subtle and most people will not be able to tell which one was used. An advantage of using sugar over honey is that most kitchens usually have sugar on hand but not always honey. As with Basic Crust Number 1, Basic Crust Number 2 is crispy on the outside and moist on the inside.

The New York Style Pizza Crust is drier and crispier since no olive oil is used except to grease the bowl. It is also a less sweet crust since neither sugar nor honey is used.

The Whole-Wheat Pizza Crust recipe is a good combination of whole wheat flour and all-purpose flour. It has a strong flavor and a nutty, chewy texture because of the whole wheat flour which makes it a good choice for a pizza with hearty toppings. Increasing the amount of whole wheat flour while decreasing the all-purpose flour will give a crust a heavier, not quite as soft, and crisper quality.

If you want a stronger flavor you will prefer the Rye Pizza Crust, but it will not go well with all toppings. The rye flavor and the molasses give an intensity of taste. Since it is deliciously different from the usual pizza crusts it is a good idea to experiment to see what you like on top.

If you desire a very tactile experience when eating your pizza you will like the crunchy, bumpy texture of the Cornmeal Pizza Crust. This crust also comes out a little thicker than the others.

The Semolina Pizza Crust uses flour made from hard durum wheat and is good for moister toppings since it resists getting soggy.

If you do not have enough time or energy to prepare your own crusts there are several alternatives available. Premixed pizza dough can purchased and all you have to do is roll it out to the size you want for your pizza. There are prepared pizza crusts that are already spread out and all you do is add the sauce and toppings of your choice and then bake.

For something a little different, you might want to try one of the prepared pizza crusts that come with a variety of seasonings, oils, and cheeses already included in the crusts.

Mix, knead, let rise, punch down, roll out . . . and then cover with sauce and toppings, bake, and enjoy.

Basic Pizza Crust Number 1

½ teaspoon honey
1 cup warm water
1 package (¼ ounce) active dry yeast
2¾ cups all-purpose flour

½ teaspoon salt
1 tablespoon extra-virgin olive oil
olive oil for greasing bowl

Stir honey into warm water and mix well. Slowly add yeast to water, mixing thoroughly, until yeast dissolves. Set aside in a warm area for approximately 5 minutes, until yeast begins to foam.

Combine flour, salt, and 1 tablespoon olive oil. Mix slightly in an electric mixer with a dough hook or in a food processor with a steel blade or by hand with a wooden spoon. Add yeast mixture and mix in an electric mixer for approximately 3 minutes or in a processor for 5 to 10 seconds or by hand for 3 to 5 minutes until smooth dough is formed.

Working on a lightly floured surface, knead dough by pressing heels of hand into dough and pushing away. Rotate dough one-quarter turn and repeat pressing and pushing with heels of hand, occasionally folding dough onto itself as it is kneaded. If dough feels sticky, sprinkle flour, a teaspoonful or two at a time, into dough. Continue kneading until dough is smooth.

Place dough in a bowl greased with olive oil, turning dough until entire surface is covered with olive oil. Cover with a light cloth towel and put bowl in a warm, draft-free place. Let dough rise until it doubles in size, about 1 hour. To test if dough has doubled, lightly and quickly press two finger tips ½-inch down into the dough. If the indentation from the finger tips remain, dough has doubled in size.

Punch down dough by placing fist into center of the dough and then pulling edges of the dough into the center and turning over.

Let dough sit for 5 minutes and then knead for 1 to 2 minutes on a lightly floured surface.

Divide dough in half and roll out each half into a circle 12 inches in diameter.

Yield: 2 12-inch round pizza crusts

Basic Pizza Crust Number 2

1 tablespoon sugar
1 cup warm water
1 package (¼ ounce) active dry yeast
3¼ cups all-purpose flour

1 teaspoon salt
¼ cup extra-virgin olive oil
olive oil for greasing bowl

Stir sugar into warm water and mix well. Slowly add yeast to water, mixing thoroughly, until yeast dissolves. Set aside in a warm area for approximately 5 minutes, until yeast begins to foam.

Combine flour, salt, and ¼ cup olive oil. Mix slightly in an electric mixer with a dough hook or in a food processor with a steel blade or by hand with a wooden spoon. Add yeast mixture and mix in an electric mixer for approximately 3 minutes or in a processor for 5 to 10 seconds or by hand for 3 to 5 minutes until smooth dough is formed.

Working on a lightly floured surface, knead dough by pressing heels of hand into dough and pushing away. Rotate dough one-quarter turn and repeat pressing and pushing with heels of hand, occasionally folding dough onto itself as it is kneaded. If dough feels sticky, sprinkle flour, a teaspoonful or two at a time, into dough. Continue kneading until dough is smooth.

Place dough in a bowl greased with olive oil, turning dough until entire surface is covered with olive oil. Cover with a light cloth towel and put bowl in a warm, draft-free place. Let dough rise until it doubles in size, about 1 hour. To test if dough has doubled, lightly and quickly press two finger tips ½-inch down into the dough. If the indentation from the finger tips remain, dough has doubled in size.

Punch down dough by placing fist into center of the dough and then pulling edges of the dough into the center and turning over.

Let dough sit for 5 minutes and then knead for 1 to 2 minutes on a lightly floured surface. Divide dough in half and roll out each half into a circle 12 inches in diameter.

Yield: 2 12-inch round pizza crusts

New York Style Pizza Crust

1 package (¼ ounce) active dry yeast
1 cup warm water
3¼ cups all-purpose flour

¾ teaspoon salt
olive oil for greasing bowl

Slowly add yeast to water, mixing thoroughly, until yeast dissolves. Set aside in a warm area for approximately 5 minutes, until yeast begins to foam.

Combine flour and salt. Mix slightly in an electric mixer with a dough hook or in a food processor with a steel blade or by hand with a wooden spoon. Add yeast mixture and mix in an electric mixer for approximately 3 minutes or in a processor for 5 to 10 seconds or by hand for 3 to 5 minutes until smooth dough is formed.

Working on a lightly floured surface, knead dough by pressing heels of hand into dough and pushing away. Rotate dough one-quarter turn and repeat processing and pushing with heels of hand, occasionally folding dough onto itself as it is kneaded. If dough feels sticky, sprinkle flour, a teaspoonful or two at a time, into dough. Continue kneading until dough is smooth.

Place dough in a bowl greased with olive oil, turning dough until entire surface is covered with olive oil. Cover with a light cloth towel and put bowl in a warm, draft-free place. Let dough rise until it doubles in size, about 1 hour. To test if dough has doubled, lightly and quickly press two finger tips ½-inch down into the dough. If the indentation from the finger tips remain, dough has doubled in size.

Punch down dough by placing fist into center of the dough and then pulling edges of the dough into the center and turning over.

Let dough sit for 5 minutes and then knead for 1 to 2 minutes on a lightly floured surface.

Divide dough in half and roll out each half into a circle 12 inches in diameter.

Yield: 2 12-inch round pizza crusts

Whole-Wheat Pizza Crust

1 tablespoon honey
1¼ cups warm water
1 package (¼ ounce) active dry yeast
2 cups whole wheat flour

1¾ cups all-purpose flour
1 teaspoon salt
¼ cup extra-virgin olive oil
olive oil for greasing bowl

Stir honey into warm water and mix well. Slowly add yeast to water, mixing thoroughly, until yeast dissolves. Set aside in a warm area for approximately 5 minutes, until yeast begins to foam.

Combine whole wheat flour, all-purpose flour, salt, and ¼ cup olive oil. Mix slightly in an electric mixer with a dough hook or in a food processor with a steel blade or by hand with a wooden spoon. Add yeast mixture and mix in an electric mixer for approximately 3 minutes or in a processor for 5 to 10 seconds or by hand for 3 to 5 minutes until smooth dough is formed.

Working on a lightly floured surface, knead dough by pressing heels of hand into dough and pushing away. Rotate dough one-quarter turn and repeat pressing and pushing with heels of hand, occasionally folding dough onto itself as it is kneaded. If dough feels sticky, sprinkle flour, a teaspoonful or two at a time, into dough. Continue kneading until dough is smooth.

Place dough in a bowl greased with olive oil, turning dough until entire surface is covered with olive oil. Cover with a light cloth towel and put bowl in a warm, draft-free place. Let dough rise until it doubles in size, about 1 hour. To test if dough has doubled, lightly and quickly press two finger tips ½-inch down into the dough. If the indentation from the finger tips remain, dough has doubled in size.

Punch down dough by placing fist into center of the dough and then pulling edges of the dough into the center and turning over.

Let dough sit for 5 minutes and then knead for 1 to 2 minutes on a lightly floured surface.

Divide dough in half and roll out each half into a circle 12 inches in diameter.

Yield: 2 12-inch round pizza crusts

Rye Pizza Crust

1 teaspoon honey
¾ cup warm water
1 package (¼ ounce) active dry yeast
1 cup rye flour
1⅓ cups all-purpose flour

½ teaspoon salt
2 tablespoons molasses
2 tablespoons extra-virgin olive oil
olive oil for greasing bowl

Stir honey into warm water and mix well. Slowly add yeast to water, mixing thoroughly, until yeast dissolves. Set aside in a warm area for approximately 5 minutes, until yeast begins to foam.

Combine rye flour, all-purpose flour, salt, molasses, and 2 tablespoons olive oil. Mix slightly in an electric mixer with a dough hook or in a food processor with a steel blade or by hand with a wooden spoon. Add yeast mixture and mix in an electric mixer for approximately 3 minutes or in a processor for 5 to 10 seconds or by hand for 3 to 5 minutes until smooth dough is formed.

Working on a lightly floured surface, knead dough by pressing heels of hand into dough and pushing away. Rotate dough one-quarter turn and repeat pressing and pushing with heels of hand, occasionally folding dough onto itself as it is kneaded. If dough feels sticky, sprinkle flour, a teaspoonful or two at a time, into dough. Continue kneading until dough is smooth.

Place dough in a bowl greased with olive oil, turning dough until entire surface is covered with olive oil. Cover with a light cloth towel and put bowl in a warm, draft-free place. Let dough rise until it doubles in size, about 1 hour. To test if dough has doubled, lightly and quickly press two finger tips ½-inch down into the dough. If the indentation from the finger tips remain, dough has doubled in size.

Punch down dough by placing fist into center of the dough and then pulling edges of the dough into the center and turning over.

Let dough sit for 5 minutes and then knead for 1 to 2 minutes on a lightly floured surface.

Divide dough in half and roll out each half into a circle 12 inches in diameter.

Yield: 2 12-inch round pizza crusts

Cornmeal Pizza Crust

½ teaspoon honey
1 cup warm water
1 package (¼ ounce) active dry yeast
1 cup white or yellow cornmeal

1¾ cups all-purpose flour
½ teaspoon salt
2 tablespoons extra-virgin olive oil
olive oil for greasing bowl

Stir honey into warm water and mix well. Slowly add yeast to water, mixing thoroughly, until yeast dissolves. Set aside in a warm area for approximately 5 minutes, until yeast begins to foam.

Combine cornmeal, all-purpose flour, salt, and 2 tablespoons olive oil. Mix slightly in an electric mixer with a dough hook or in a food processor with a steel blade or by hand with a wooden spoon. Add yeast mixture and mix in an electric mixer for approximately 3 minutes or in a processor for 5 to 10 seconds or by hand for 3 to 5 minutes until smooth dough is formed.

Working on a lightly floured surface, knead dough by pressing heels of hand into dough and pushing away. Rotate dough one-quarter turn and repeat pressing and pushing with heels of hand, occasionally folding dough onto itself as it is kneaded. If dough feels sticky, sprinkle flour, a teaspoonful or two at a time, into dough. Continue kneading until dough is smooth.

Place dough in a bowl greased with olive oil, turning dough until entire surface is covered with olive oil. Cover with a light cloth towel and put bowl in a warm, draft-free place. Let dough rise until it doubles in size, about 1 hour. To test if dough has doubled, lightly and quickly press two finger tips ½-inch down into the dough. If the indentation from the finger tips remain, dough has doubled in size.

Punch down dough by placing fist into center of the dough and then pulling edges of the dough into the center and turning over.

Let dough sit for 5 minutes and then knead for 1 to 2 minutes on a lightly floured surface.

Divide dough in half and roll out each half into a circle 12 inches in diameter.

Yield: 2 12-inch round pizza crusts

Semolina Pizza Crust

1 teaspoon sugar
1 cup warm water
1 package (¼ ounce) active dry yeast
2½ cups semolina flour

1 teaspoon salt
1 tablespoon extra-virgin olive oil
olive oil for greasing bowl

Stir sugar into warm water and mix well. Slowly add yeast to water, mixing thoroughly, until yeast dissolves. Set aside in a warm area for approximately 5 minutes, until yeast begins to foam.

Combine semolina flour, salt, and 1 tablespoon olive oil. Mix slightly in an electric mixer with a dough hook or in a food processor with a steel blade or by hand with a wooden spoon. Add yeast mixture and mix in an electric mixer for approximately 3 minutes or in a processor for 5 to 10 seconds or by hand for 3 to 5 minutes until smooth dough is formed.

Working on a lightly floured surface, knead dough by pressing heels of hand into dough and pushing away. Rotate dough one-quarter turn and repeat pressing and pushing with heels of hand, occasionally folding dough onto itself as it is kneaded. If dough feels sticky, sprinkle flour, a teaspoonful or two at a time, into dough. Continue kneading until dough is smooth.

Place dough in a bowl greased with olive oil, turning dough until entire surface is covered with olive oil. Cover with a light cloth towel and put bowl in a warm, draft-free place. Let dough rise until it doubles in size, about 1 hour. To test if dough has doubled, lightly and quickly press two finger tips ½-inch down into the dough. If the indentation from the finger tips remain, dough has doubled in size.

Punch down dough by placing fist into center of the dough and then pulling edges of the dough into the center and turning over.

Let dough sit for 5 minutes and then knead for 1 to 2 minutes on a lightly floured surface.

Divide dough in half and roll out each half into a circle 12 inches in diameter.

Yield: 2 12-inch round pizza crusts

Hearty Pizzas

Hot Sausage and Pepper Pizza

Irene McClure
Kirkwood, Missouri

1 prepared 12-inch unbaked pizza crust
2 cups crumbled cooked hot Italian sausage
12 cherry tomatoes, cut into halves
1 red pepper, sliced

1 green pepper, sliced
½ cup chopped scallions
1 tablespoon chopped fresh basil
½ cup shredded Monterey Jack cheese
¼ cup grated Parmesan cheese

Preheat oven to 425 degrees F.

Spread sausage, tomatoes, red pepper, green pepper, scallions, and basil on unbaked pizza crust. Sprinkle Monterey Jack cheese and Parmesan cheese over top.

Bake at 425 degrees F for 15 to 20 minutes, until cheeses have melted and crust is golden brown.

Cut into 6 or 8 slices.

Cheese-Steak Pizza

Christina Segal
Newton, Massachusetts

1 prepared 12-inch unbaked pizza crust
1½ cups prepared mashed potatoes
2 cups cooked pieces of steak
1 cup cooked corn
½ cup cooked peas

1 garlic clove, crushed
3 tablespoons steak sauce
½ cup shredded Monterey Jack cheese
½ cup shredded mozzarella cheese

Preheat oven to 425 degrees F.

Spread mashed potatoes on unbaked pizza crust. Place steak pieces, corn, peas, garlic, steak sauce, Monterey Jack cheese, and mozzarella cheese over top.

Bake at 425 degrees F for 15 to 20 minutes, until cheeses have melted and crust is golden brown.

Cut into 6 or 8 slices.

Lana Turner was "discovered" while eating a hamburger at a hamburger stand across the street from Hollywood High School on Sunset Boulevard where she was a student.

Natalie Portman, the star in the title role in the Broadway play "The Diary of Anne Frank," was discovered by a scout as she sat in a pizza parlor on Long Island, east of New York City.

Sausage and Potato Pizza

Matt Woodall
Commack Village, Arkansas

1 prepared 12-inch unbaked pizza
crust
6 small red potatoes
1 pound sausage
2 red peppers, sliced

1 teaspoon parsley
½ teaspoon basil
¼ teaspoon paprika
1½ cups shredded mozzarella

Boil potatoes until almost soft. Drain. Slice potatoes into ¼-inch thick slices. Set aside.

Preheat oven to 425 degrees F.

Fry sausage until almost done. Drain and crumble into small pieces. Return crumbled sausage to frying pan, add potato slices and pepper slices, and cook over medium heat for about 5 to 10 minutes until pepper slices are soft. Drain well. Mix in parsley, basil, and paprika. Spread on unbaked pizza crust. Sprinkle mozzarella cheese over top.

Bake at 425 degrees F for 15 to 20 minutes, until cheese has melted and crust is golden brown.

Cut into 6 or 8 slices.

Parsley

One of the oldest spices in use today is parsley, not only for eating but also for well being.

Crowns made from parsley were worn by guests at Greek banquets to give them a serene look and to stimulate their appetite.

It was not too long ago that parsley was only available if you grew it yourself, since parsley has been produced and sold commercially in large quantities just in the last 25 to 30 years.

Most of the parsley that is grown in the United States comes from California and Texas.

Spicy Chicken and Bean Pizza

Myra Younger
Sand Springs, Oklahoma

1 prepared 12-inch unbaked pizza crust
3 tomatoes, diced
3 cups shredded cooked chicken
1 15-ounce can pinto beans, drained

$\frac{1}{4}$ to $\frac{1}{2}$ cup chopped jalapeño peppers
2 large onions, sliced
$\frac{3}{4}$ cup hot salsa
1 cup shredded Cheddar cheese
sour cream

Preheat oven to 425 degrees F.

Spread tomatoes, chicken, pinto beans, jalapeño peppers, and onions on unbaked pizza crust. Cover with salsa and Cheddar cheese.

Bake at 425 degrees F for 15 to 20 minutes, until cheese has melted and crust is golden brown. Serve with sour cream.

Cut into 6 or 8 slices.

The earth is going to be destroyed by a massive meteor heading straight for us in the movie "Deep Impact."

The news is so shocking that it causes a comet expert, played by Charles Martin Smith, eating a slice of pizza at his computer to drop his pizza. He is really shocked!

Barbecue Pizza

Joyce Nordin
Bloomington, Minnesota

1 prepared 12-inch unbaked pizza crust
$\frac{1}{2}$ cup barbecue sauce
2 cups barbecued chicken pieces
2 cups chopped mushrooms

1$\frac{1}{2}$ cups chopped broccoli
$\frac{1}{2}$ cup tomato sauce
1$\frac{1}{2}$ cups shredded Monterey Jack cheese

Preheat oven to 425 degrees F.

Spread barbecue sauce on unbaked pizza crust. Place chicken, mushrooms, broccoli, tomato sauce, and Monterey Jack cheese over top.

Bake at 425 degrees F for 15 to 20 minutes, until cheese has melted and crust is golden brown.

Cut into 6 or 8 slices.

Pizza is good for you. The cheeses provide protein, calcium, vitamins, and minerals. The crust has complex carbohydrates and the vegetables give vitamins and fiber with a minimum of calories.

In fact, a single slice of well-accessorized pizza includes all four food groups: grains, vegetables, dairy, and meat.

Beyond Sausage and Pepperoni

In addition to the sausages and pepperoni that are often found on pizza, there are many other kinds of meat that can make your pizza tasty and enjoyable. Some of these meats are:

- lauganega sausage
- kielbasa
- smoked kielbasa
- Canadian bacon
- pork roll
- bratwurst

- knockwurst
- ground beef
- capicolla ham
- ground turkey meat
- spicy chorizo

- hot calabrese
- pancetta
- pastrami
- corned beef
- salami
- baked ham

Meatball Pizza

John Guerra
Kendall, Florida

1 prepared 12-inch unbaked pizza crust
1 pound ground beef
¼ cup olive oil
4 large tomatoes, sliced
2 red peppers, thinly sliced
1 medium onion, sliced
1 garlic clove, crushed

½ teaspoon oregano
¼ teaspoon salt
dash pepper
1 tablespoon Worcestershire sauce
1½ to 2 cups shredded mozzarella cheese
¼ cup grated Parmesan cheese

Preheat oven to 425 degrees F.

Roll ground beef into small balls and cook in olive oil until meat is cooked and then drain.

Spread tomatoes, meat balls, red peppers, onion slices, and garlic on unbaked pizza crust. Sprinkle oregano, salt, pepper, and Worcestershire sauce over top. Sprinkle mozzarella cheese and Parmesan cheese on top.

Bake at 425 degrees F for 15 to 20 minutes, until cheeses have melted and crust is golden brown.

Cut into 6 or 8 slices.

Two-Meat Two-Cheese Pizza

Stewart Moeller
Norwood, Ohio

1 prepared 12-inch unbaked pizza crust
2 large onions, sliced
1 cup mushroom slices
2 garlic cloves, crushed
1 tablespoon olive oil
1 cup thin pepperoni slices, well fried and blotted

8 ounces prosciutto, cut into pieces
1 cup spaghetti sauce
1 cup shredded Monterey Jack cheese
1½ cups shredded mozzarella cheese

Preheat oven to 425 degrees F.

Sauté onions, mushrooms, and garlic in olive oil. Drain and place on unbaked pizza crust. Place pepperoni and prosciutto on top. Cover with spaghetti sauce and sprinkle Monterey Jack cheese and mozzarella cheese over top.

Bake at 425 degrees F for 15 to 20 minutes, until cheeses have melted and crust is golden brown.

Cut into 6 or 8 slices.

The most popular topping for pizza in the United States is pepperoni while the least desired is anchovies.

Pizza Pot Pie

Leslie Lambrecht
Oak Creek, Wisconsin

amount of dough needed for 2
12-inch pizza crusts
1 cup diced onions
1½ cups diced red peppers
1½ cups diced green peppers
1½ cups sliced mushrooms
2 garlic cloves, minced
¼ cup olive oil
½ pound sausage
1 pound ground beef
1 28-ounce can tomato purée

1 6-ounce can tomato paste
1 teaspoon oregano
1 tablespoon fresh parsley
1 teaspoon salt
½ teaspoon pepper
½ cup shredded Cheddar cheese
2 cups shredded mozzarella cheese
½ cup grated Parmesan cheese
1 egg yolk mixed with 2 tablespoons
water

Sauté in a large pan onions, red peppers, green peppers, mushrooms, and garlic in olive oil for approximately 10 minutes. Remove from pan and set aside.

Put sausage and ground beef into pan and cook until done. Remove meats from pan and blot.

Drain oil from pan and return blotted meats to pan. Add vegetable mixture, tomato purée, tomato paste, oregano, parsley, salt, and pepper. Heat to boiling. Reduce heat and simmer, stirring frequently, for 10 to 15 minutes.

Pour sauce into a 9x13-inch baking pan. Sprinkle Cheddar cheese, mozzarella cheese, and Parmesan cheese over top.

Preheat oven to 350 degrees F.

Using the amount of dough that makes 2 12-inch pizza crusts, roll out dough into an 11x 15-inch rectangle.

Cover pan with unbaked pizza crust and crimp edges of crust onto edges of pan.
Brush egg yolk and water mixture on crust. Prick crust with a fork in several places.
Place baking pan on a cookie sheet in center of oven.
Bake at 350 degrees F for 30 to 40 minutes, until crust is golden brown.
Serves 6 to 8.

Oregano

Oregano was so popular in ancient Greece that it was called "joy of the mountain."

It is a member of the mint family of plants and has leaves a little over one-half inch long. It is sold both as whole leaves and ground into small pieces.

Oregano is imported into the United States from Greece, Mexico, and Japan.

Chili Powder

Chili powder is a blend of spices—including red pepper, cumin, oregano, garlic powder, and salt—created in the Southwestern United States during the 1800s.

The hot sensation comes primarily from capcaican, the most potent chemical in cayenne peppers.

Besides giving a definite flavor to many dishes, chili powder can also stimulate the appetite.

Bacon and Egg Pizza

Patrick Koch
College Park, Georgia

1 prepared 12-inch unbaked pizza crust
2 tablespoons Dijon mustard
1 pound bacon, cooked crisp and broken into small pieces

8 to 10 plum tomatoes, sliced
4 large scrambled eggs
1 cup cottage cheese
½ cup shredded mozzarella cheese

Preheat oven to 425 degrees F.

Spread mustard on unbaked pizza crust. Bake at 425 degrees F for 12 minutes.

Sprinkle bacon pieces, tomato slices, scrambled eggs, cottage cheese, and mozzarella cheese on crust.

Bake at 425 degrees F for 6 to 8 minutes more, until mozzarella cheese has melted and crust is golden brown.

Cut into 6 or 8 slices.

As part of the United States military activities in Bosnia, a logistical support base was set up in the tiny village of Taszar in Hungary. To give the 4,000 American GIs a feeling of home, the army set up on base a gym, a movie theater, a beer tent, and, of course, a pizza parlor.

Ham and Peas Pizza

Leona Rizzo
Milford, Connecticut

1 prepared 12-inch unbaked pizza crust
1 tablespoon olive oil
8 ounces prosciutto

1 cup fresh peas
10 black olives, pitted and sliced
3 large tomatoes, sliced
1 cup shredded mozzarella cheese

Preheat oven to 425 degrees F.

Spread olive oil on crust. Arrange prosciutto, peas, black olives, and tomato slices on crust. Sprinkle mozzarella cheese over top.

Bake at 425 degrees F for 15 to 20 minutes, until cheese has melted and crust is golden brown.

Cut into 6 or 8 slices.

In the book *McNally's Puzzle* by Lawrence Sanders, Archy McNally is the intrepid, fun-loving, and fine food aficionado who is the entire Department of Discreet Inquiries at his father's law firm in Palm Beach, Florida.

His task as investigator takes him to many different places to meet with many different people.

So it comes as no surprise to readers to find Archy lunching at a pizza joint appropriately named the Pizza Joint, dining on the King Kong Special, a pizza covered with cheese, eggplant, sausage, anchovies, and button mushrooms.

Chicken, Walnut, and Gorgonzola Pizza

Jennifer Pickens
Bartlett, Tennessee

1 prepared 12-inch unbaked pizza crust
1 cup chopped Vidalia onions
1½ cups chopped mushrooms
2 tablespoons olive oil

2 cups diced cooked chicken breast
½ cup chopped walnuts
½ teaspoon sage
¾ cup crumbled Gorgonzola cheese

Preheat oven to 425 degrees F.

Sauté onions and mushrooms in olive oil until onions are golden brown. Add chicken and continue cooking for 4 to 5 minutes more. Remove from heat and spread on unbaked pizza crust. Sprinkle walnuts, sage, and Gorgonzola cheese over top.

Bake at 425 degrees F for 15 to 20 minutes, until cheese has melted and crust is golden brown.

Cut into 6 or 8 slices.

There are over 62,000 restaurants in the United States serving pizza, including neighborhood mom-and-pop pizzerias, gourmet cafés, large restaurants, and all those places run by regional and giant national chains. That's a lot of pies!

California Pizza Kitchen
Los Angeles, California

Makes 2 9-inch pizzas

BBQ Chicken (recipe follows)
cornmeal, semolina or flour for
handling
½ cup favorite BBQ sauce (we use a
spicy-sweet sauce)
2 tablespoons shredded smoked
Gouda cheese

2 cups shredded mozzarella cheese
Basic Pizza Dough (recipe follows)
¼ small red onion, sliced into
⅛-inch pieces
2 tablespoons chopped fresh
cilantro

Place the pizza stone in the center of the oven and preheat to 500 degrees F for one hour before cooking pizzas.

Use a large spoon to spread ¼ cup BBQ sauce evenly over the surface of the prepared dough within the rim. Sprinkle 1 tablespoon smoked Gouda cheese over the sauce. Cover with ¾ cup shredded mozzarella.

Distribute half the chicken pieces evenly over the cheese (approximately 18 pieces). Place approximately 18 to 20 pieces of red onion over the surface. Sprinkle an additional ¼ cup mozzarella over the top of the pizza.

Transfer the pizza to the oven; bake until the crust is crisp and golden and the cheese at the center is bubbly, 8 to 10 minutes. When the pizza is cooked, carefully remove it from the oven; sprinkle 1 tablespoon cilantro over the hot surface. Slice and serve.

Repeat with remaining ingredients for a second pizza. (The two pizzas may be prepared simultaneously if you are careful in placing the pizzas at opposite corners of your pizza stone.)

BBQ Chicken

10 ounces boneless/skinless chicken breasts, cut into ¾-inch cubes
1 tablespoon olive oil

2 tablespoons favorite BBQ sauce (we use a spicy-sweet sauce)

In a large frying pan, cook the chicken in olive oil over medium-high heat until just cooked, 5 to 6 minutes. Do not overcook. Set aside in the refrigerator until chilled through.

Once chilled, coat the chicken with 2 tablespoons BBQ sauce; set aside in the refrigerator.

Basic Pizza Dough

Makes dough for 2 9-inch pizzas.

1 teaspoon yeast
½ cup plus 1 tablespoon warm water (105 degrees to 110 degrees F)
1½ cups bread flour or all-purpose flour

2 teaspoons sugar
1 teaspoon salt
1 tablespoon extra-virgin olive oil plus 1 teaspoon for coating

Honey-Wheat Pizza Dough

1 teaspoon yeast
½ cup plus 1 teaspoon warm water
(105 degrees to 110 degrees F)
1 cup bread flour
½ cup whole wheat flour

5 teaspoons clover honey
1 teaspoon salt
1 tablespoon extra-virgin olive oil
plus 1 teaspoon for coating

Dissolve the yeast in the water and set aside for 5 to 10 minutes. Be sure that the water is not hot: temperatures of 120 degrees F and above will kill the yeast, and your dough will not rise.

If using an upright electric mixer, such as a KitchenAid, use the mixing paddle attachment because the batch size is too small for the dough hook to be effective. Combine all the ingredients (except the additional teaspoon of olive oil) and combine them with the dissolved yeast in the mixing bowl. Do not pour the salt directly into the yeast water because this would kill some of the yeast. Allow these 2 ingredients to mix gradually; use the lowest 2 speeds to mix the dough. Mix for 2 to 3 minutes, until the dough is smooth and elastic. Overmixing will produce tough, rubbery dough, and friction will cause dough to rise too fast.

If using a food processor, use a dough "blade" made of plastic rather than the sharp steel knife attachment which would cut the gluten strands and ruin the consistency of the dough. Otherwise, proceed as above. Be especially cautious not to mix too long with a food processor because the temperature resulting from the friction of mixing could easily exceed 120 degrees F, killing your yeast. Mix only until a smooth dough ball is formed.

If mixing by hand, place the dry ingredients in a 4- to 6-quart mixing bowl; make a well in the middle and pour in the liquids (reserving the teaspoon of olive oil). Use a wooden spoon to combine the ingredients. Once initial mixing is done, you can lightly oil your hands and begin kneading the dough; knead for 5 minutes.

When done the dough should be slightly tacky (that is, it should be barely beyond sticking to your hands).

Lightly oil the dough ball and the interior of a 1-quart glass bowl. Place the dough ball in the bowl and seal the bowl with clear food wrap; seal air tight. Set aside at room temperature (70–80 degrees) to rise until double in bulk, about $1\frac{1}{2}$ to 2 hours.

The dough could be used at this point, but it will not be that wonderful, chewy, flavorful dough that it will later become.

Punch down the dough, re-form a nice round ball and return it to the same bowl; cover again with clear food wrap. Place the bowl in the refrigerator overnight, covered airtight.

About 2 hours before you are ready to assemble your pizza, remove the dough from the refrigerator. Use a sharp knife to divide the dough into 2 equal portions or 4 equal portions if making appetizer-sized pizza or if smaller, 6-inch pizzas are desired.

Roll the smaller doughs into round balls on a smooth, clean surface; be sure to seal any holes by pinching or rolling.

Place the newly formed dough balls in a glass casserole dish, spaced far enough apart to allow for each to double in size. Seal the top of the dish airtight with clear food wrap. Set aside at room temperature until the dough balls have doubled in size (about 2 hours). They should be smooth and puffy.

To stretch and form the dough for pizza:

1) Sprinkle a medium dusting of flour over a 12x12-inch clean, smooth surface. Use a metal spatula or dough scraper to carefully remove a dough ball from the glass casserole dish, being very careful to preserve its round shape. Flour the dough liberally. Place the floured dough on the floured smooth surface.

2) Use your hands or a rolling pin to press the dough down forming a flat circle about $\frac{1}{2}$ inch thick. Pinch the dough between your fingers all around the edge of circle, forming a lip or rim that rises about $\frac{1}{4}$ inch above the center surface of the dough. You may continue this outward stretching motion of the hands until you have reached a 9-inch diameter pizza dough. Or, for the more adventurous, proceed to Step 3.

3) Here comes the tricky part. Place the rimmed dough on the backs of your hands with your fingers spread about an inch apart. The edge of the dough should rest on the backs of the second knuckles of both hands.

4) Wind up for the toss by rotating your hands $\frac{1}{4}$ revolution in the opposite direction from the way you will be spinning the dough. To wind up: Both hands align with your chin; your hands turn so that your right hand is the farthest away with palm facing (thumb up). Your left hand should be closer to you with the thumb down.

5) Stretch the dough out slightly and spin the dough upward by flicking your hands outward in opposite directions. The motion is like both hands are quickly losing an arm wrestling match. Your left hand arcs up and out to the left at the same time your right hand arcs up and out to the right. Catch the spinning dough on the backs of your hands. (Or pick it up off the floor and try again—just kidding!) If necessary, re-position your hands and repeat the toss until you've formed a 9-inch circular dough.

To dress the pizza:

1) Lightly sprinkle cornmeal, semolina or flour over the surface of a wooden pizza peel. Arrange the stretched dough over the floured peel surface. Work quickly (following one of the pizza recipes) to dress the pizza so that the dough won't become soggy or sticky from sauces and toppings.

2) When you are ready to transfer the pizza to the pizza stone in the preheated oven, grasp the handle of the peel and execute a very small test jerk to verify that the pizza will come easily off the peel. If the dough doesn't move freely, carefully lift the edges of the dough and try to rotate it by hand. Extreme cases may require that you toss more flour under the dough edges.

Veggie Pizzas

Ratatouille Pizza

Andria Harrington
Troy, New York

1 prepared 12-inch unbaked pizza crust
2 tablespoons olive oil
3 tablespoons lemon juice
½ teaspoon thyme
1 garlic clove, minced
1 large eggplant, cut lengthwise into ½-inch slices
salt

3 medium zucchini, cut lengthwise into ½-inch slices
1 large red pepper, seeded and sliced
1 large green pepper, seeded and sliced
1 Vidalia onion, cut into ½-inch rounds
1 large tomato, sliced
¼ cup fresh parsley, minced

Preheat barbecue grill to medium-high heat.

Mix together olive oil, lemon juice, thyme, and garlic. Set aside.

Sprinkle eggplant slices on both sides with salt. Let sit for 15 minutes, rinse, and pat dry.

Place eggplant, zucchini, red pepper, green pepper, onion rounds, and tomato slices on a grill screen and place on grill. Brush with lemon juice sauce and grill for about 4 to 6 minutes on each side or until slightly charred.

Remove from grill and arrange vegetables on unbaked pizza crust. Sprinkle with parsley.

Bake pizza for 10 minutes on a tile on a covered barbecue grill or bake in a preheated 400 degree F oven for 10 to 15 minutes.

Cut into 6 or 8 slices.

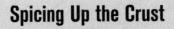

Spicing Up the Crust

Many herbs, spices, seeds, nuts, vegetables, cheeses, and meats can be added to pizza dough to create a variety of very tasty and unusual crusts.

These items (chopped or grated as necessary) should be added to the dough just before the final kneading, after the dough has been punched down and allowed to sit for 5 minutes.

Here are a few savory suggestions, which can be used alone or in combinations.

- paprika
- dill weed
- chives
- parsley
- scallions
- garlic
- rosemary
- anise
- cumin seeds
- sunflower seeds
- celery seeds
- sesame seeds
- poppy seeds
- fennel seeds

- walnuts
- pecans
- almonds
- peanuts
- chili peppers
- sun-dried tomatoes
- olives
- dried cranberries
- pimentos
- lemon zest
- Cheddar cheese
- provolone cheese

- Romano cheese
- Parmesan cheese
- mozzarella cheese
- fontina cheese
- feta cheese
- pepperoni
- sausage
- salami
- prosciutto
- bacon
- capicolla ham
- anchovies

Artichoke Hearts and Spinach Pizza

Lisa Castillo
Avra, Arizona

1 prepared 12-inch unbaked pizza crust
1 10-ounce package of frozen chopped spinach
1 large mild onion, sliced
1 tablespoon olive oil
1 cup crushed cherry tomatoes

10 to 12 artichoke hearts, sliced in half
¾ cup shredded low-fat or nonfat ricotta cheese
1 cup cherry tomato halves
1 cup shredded low-fat or nonfat mozzarella cheese

Preheat oven to 425 degrees F.

Cook spinach and drain well. Set aside.

Sauté onion slices in olive oil and then arrange on unbaked pizza crust. Cover with crushed cherry tomatoes, artichoke hearts, cooked spinach, ricotta cheese, and cherry tomato halves. Sprinkle mozzarella cheese over top.

Bake at 425 degrees F for 15 to 20 minutes, until cheeses have melted and crust is golden brown.

Cut into 6 or 8 slices.

When the Boy's Choir of St. Thomas Church of Leipzig, Germany, was in New York City for a performance recently, the 80 boys went to John's Pizzeria on West 44th Street and, following their meal, lined up on the balcony and sang two works, one by Mendelsohn and one by Bach.

Everyone, from bartenders and pizza bakers to all the patrons, were transfixed by the performance and gave the choir a rousing standing ovation.

The Interplanetary Eggplant Pizza

Kathie Mainzer and Carol Downs
Bella Luna Restaurant
Boston, Massachusetts

Makes 2 16-inch pizzas

Pizza Dough (recipe follows)
Pizza Sauce (recipe follows)
2 cups fresh spinach, ripped into
medium sized pieces

2 cups Italian breaded eggplant
(available in supermarkets)
1 cup sun-dried tomatoes
1½ pounds shredded mozzarella
cheese

Cover Pizza Dough (already pressed into shape) with a layer of Pizza Sauce. Evenly distribute spinach, breaded eggplant, and sun-dried tomatoes over each pizza. Spread half of mozzarella cheese on each pizza.

Cook in oven for 10 to 15 minutes, or until crust is golden and firm to the touch.

Do not overcook or the pizza will be dry in the middle.

Cut immediately and serve. Bon Appetit!

Pizza Dough

1 cake yeast
1⅓ cups water
1 teaspoon sugar
1 teaspoon salt

2 tablespoons corn oil
4 cups sifted all-purpose flour
cornmeal

Thoroughly mix yeast and cold water in a bowl. Add sugar, salt, oil, and mix again. Add flour and knead for 10 minutes. Squeeze all air out of dough and shape into round, bowl-like shape. Cover with damp cloth and let rise for 2 hours. To preserve dough for the next day, place in refrigerator. When you are ready to cook it, preheat oven to 475 degrees.

Spread cornmeal on flat surface. Cut dough into 2 equal pieces and place on cornmeal. Using your hands or a rolling pin, spread each piece flat, pressing outward with the palms of your hands to form a circle approximately 15 inches in diameter.

Pizza Sauce

2 cans whole tomatoes (28 ounces)
2 cups water
1 tablespoon oregano
1½ tablespoons basil
3 cloves garlic, pressed
2½ ounces olive oil

½ cup grated Parmesan cheese
1 tablespoon black pepper
¾ tablespoon salt
1¾ tablespoons sugar
2 tablespoons dry red wine

Combine tomatoes and water in large, heavy saucepan. Bring to a boil over low heat and let simmer for 30 minutes. Add remaining ingredients, stir, and simmer another 30 minutes.

Be careful to use low heat, and stir the sauce frequently so that it doesn't burn.

Madeline Giles
Lafayette, Colorado

1 prepared 12-inch unbaked pizza crust
1 cup shredded mozzarella cheese
1 large Portobello mushroom, chopped
2 medium onions, sliced
1 red pepper, chopped

1 green pepper, chopped
1 yellow pepper, chopped
2 cups chopped broccoli
½ cup shredded Cheddar cheese
¼ cup grated Romano cheese
¼ cup grated Parmesan cheese

Preheat oven to 425 degrees F.

Spread ½ cup mozzarella cheese on crust. Arrange mushroom, onions, red pepper, green pepper, yellow pepper, and broccoli over top. Sprinkle remaining ½ cup mozzarella cheese, Cheddar cheese, Romano cheese, and Parmesan cheese over vegetables.

Bake at 425 degrees F for 15 to 20 minutes, until cheeses have melted and crust is golden brown.

Cut into 6 or 8 slices.

The Pizza Hut restaurant chain is the largest buyer in the world of mozzarella cheese.

Roasted Garlic and Vegetable Pizza

Fred Capriani
Wilkinsburg, Pennsylvania

1 prepared 12-inch unbaked pizza crust
1 Roasted Garlic Head (recipe follows)
1 medium zucchini, thinly sliced
2 cups broccoli florettes

10 sun-dried tomatoes, cut into strips
1 teaspoon oregano
1 teaspoon basil
½ cup shredded fontina cheese
1 cup shredded mozzarella cheese

Preheat oven to 425 degrees F.

Spread Roasted Garlic Head on unbaked pizza crust. Place zucchini, broccoli, and sun-dried tomatoes over garlic. Sprinkle oregano and basil on top. Cover with fontina and mozzarella cheeses.

Bake at 425 degrees F for 15 to 20 minutes, until cheeses have melted and crust is golden brown.

Cut into 6 or 8 slices.

Roasted Garlic Head

1 whole garlic head
water or chicken stock

1 to 2 tablespoons olive oil

Preheat oven to 350 degrees F.

Cut top off of garlic head, exposing cloves. Place in a small baking dish and add enough water or stock to come one-third of the way up the side of the garlic head. Drizzle olive oil over the exposed cloves.

Cover with aluminum foil and bake at 350 degrees F for about 1 hour, until garlic is soft and tender.

Everyone knows about sausage, pepperoni, mushroom, anchovy, green pepper, and onion toppings for pizza.

But what about fiddlehead fern pizza?

You can be excused if you have never heard of fiddlehead ferns—a wild plant that has an asparagus-artichoke like flavor—or, for that matter, fiddlehead fern pizza.

If you want to try fiddlehead fern pizza it's not something you can just go down to your local pizzeria and order.

You can, however, contact R.S.V.P. pizza restaurant in Waitsfield, Vermont, which has an overnight mail order pizza business, offering a variety of pizzas.

Fiddlefern pizza is available from R.S.V.P. for about three weeks every May when the fiddlehead fern passes through its edible stage. Otherwise, you have to wait until next year.

Another specialty pizza available from R.S.V.P. is a heart-shaped pie for Valentine's Day.

Sautéed Vegetable Pizza

Hannah De Martini
Alameda, California

1 prepared 12-inch unbaked pizza crust
2 medium eggplants
salt
2 tablespoons olive oil
3 shallots, sliced thin
1 red pepper, sliced
1 yellow pepper, sliced

1 large Portobello mushroom, sliced
1½ cups non-fat ricotta cheese
½ teaspoon marjoram
¼ teaspoon salt
pepper
¼ cup crumbled Gorgonzola or blue cheese

Cut eggplants into thin slices, coat one side with salt, and let sit for 10 to 15 minutes. Turn over, coat other side with salt, and let sit another 10 to 15 minutes. Rinse well in cold water.

Preheat oven to 425 degrees F.

Sauté eggplant in olive oil. Remove from pan and blot. Set aside.

Put shallots, red pepper, yellow pepper, and mushroom slices in pan and sauté. Remove from pan and blot.

Spread ricotta cheese over unbaked pizza crust. Arrange eggplant, shallots, red pepper, yellow pepper, and mushroom slices over cheese. Sprinkle marjoram, salt, and pepper over vegetables. Sprinkle Gorgonzola or blue cheese over top.

Bake at 425 degrees F for 15 to 20 minutes, until cheeses have melted and crust is golden brown.

Cut into 6 or 8 slices.

Zito's East Sinatra Pizza
Fresh Mozzarella, Pesto, and Fresh Tomato

Anthony Zito, Tommy Bonghesan, and Jimmy Mangia
Zito's East Restaurant
New York, New York

Our pizza dough is made exclusively for Zito's East Restaurant by the famous 75-year-old Zito's bakery in Greenwich Village.

Fourteen ounces of dough are evenly spread onto a 16-inch thin round mold, continually pulling small amounts of the outer edges. Then we start flattening the center of the dough by making two fists and stretching slowly.

After the dough is evenly laid on the peel, a thin layer of our own home-made pesto is placed over the dough. We leave ¾-inch around the outside circumference of the dough. We then place thin slices (approximately ⅛-inch thick) of our freshly made mozzarella on top of the pesto and on the top of the mozzarella very thin slices of fresh tomatoes. Brush a few drops of extra-virgin olive oil on the outer crust.

We slide the pizza into our 90 plus-year-old authentic coal-fired brick oven. The temperature can reach 650-700 degrees, so the pizza must be continuously rotated to assure even cooking.

After 6 to 7 minutes, Zito's East Sinatra Pizza is "finito."

Eggplant Marinara Pizza

Liz Nielsen
Lincoln, Nebraska

1 prepared 12-inch unbaked pizza crust
1 large eggplant
salt
2 tablespoons olive oil
2 cups prepared mashed potatoes

1 teaspoon parsley
1 teaspoon tarragon
2 cups marinara sauce
½ cup grated Romano cheese
½ cup shredded Cheddar cheese

Cut eggplant into thin slices, coat one side with salt, and let sit for 10 to 15 minutes. Turn over, coat other side with salt, and let sit another 10 to 15 minutes. Rinse well in cold water.

Sauté eggplant in olive oil. Remove from pan and blot. Set aside.

Preheat oven to 425 degrees F.

Spread mashed potatoes on unbaked pizza crust. Place eggplant, parsley, and tarragon on top. Cover with marinara sauce. Sprinkle Romano cheese and Cheddar cheese on sauce.

Bake at 425 degrees F for 15 to 20 minutes, until cheeses have melted and crust is golden brown.

Cut into 6 or 8 slices.

When Barbara Walters, one of television's best known personalities, gave a birthday party for a friend at the very classy Tavern on the Green restaurant in Central Park in Manhattan, the menu included pizza with truffle shavings.

Capers and Eggplant Pizza

Venessa Dean
Alameda, New Mexico

1 prepared 12-inch unbaked pizza crust
1 large eggplant, sliced
salt
1 cup chopped celery
2 large mild onions, chopped
1 tablespoon olive oil

1 teaspoon sugar
1 tablespoon wine vinegar
1 cup tomato puree
1½ teaspoons oregano
dash pepper
2 to 3 tablespoons capers
2 cups grated mozzarella cheese

Preheat oven to 425 degrees F.

Lay out eggplant slices and salt both sides. Let sit for 15 minutes, rinse well, and drain on paper towels. Set aside.

Sauté celery and onions in olive oil until soft. Mix in sugar and vinegar and spread on unbaked pizza crust. Place eggplant slices over top. Spread tomato puree over eggplant. Sprinkle with oregano, pepper, capers, and mozzarella cheese.

Bake at 425 degrees F for 15 to 20 minutes, until cheese has melted and crust is golden brown.

Cut into 6 or 8 slices.

According to the National Restaurant Association, 61 percent of the pizza ordered in restaurants is regular thin-crust pizza, 28 percent is thick-crust pan pizza, and the remaining 11 percent is ultra-thin crust pizza.

Five-Cheese Roasted Garlic Pizza

Rhoda Boucher
Henderson, Nevada

1 prepared 12-inch unbaked pizza crust
1 cup shredded mozzarella cheese
3 heads Roasted Garlic (recipe follows)
½ cup ricotta cheese

1 teaspoon parsley
¼ teaspoon basil
¼ cup shredded Cheddar cheese
¼ cup grated Romano
¼ cup grated Parmesan

Preheat oven to 425 degrees F.

Spread ½ cup of the mozzarella cheese and Roasted Garlic on unbaked pizza crust. Cover with ricotta cheese, parsley, basil, Cheddar cheese, and remaining ½ cup of mozzarella cheese. Sprinkle Romano cheese and Parmesan cheese over top.

Bake at 425 degrees F for 15 to 20 minutes, until cheeses have melted and crust is golden brown.

Cut into 6 or 8 slices.

Roasted Garlic

3 whole garlic heads
water or chicken stock

2 to 3 tablespoons olive oil

Preheat oven to 350 degrees F.

Cut tops off of garlic heads, exposing cloves. Place in a small baking dish and add enough water to come one-third of the way up the side of the garlic heads. Drizzle olive oil over the exposed cloves.

Cover with aluminum foil and bake at 350 degrees F for about 1 hour, until garlic is soft and tender.

Remove garlic from each clove by gently squeezing.

There are many stories about the unique humor and philosophies of Lawrence Peter "Yogi" Berra, the noted Yankee player and sportscaster.

In one of those stories Yogi ordered a pizza in a restaurant and the waitress asked him if he wanted the pizza cut into six slices or eight.

Yogi replied, "Better cut it into six, I don't think I can eat eight."

Gruyère Vegetarian Pizza

Claudine Ledford
Edmond, Oklahoma

1 prepared 12-inch unbaked pizza crust
2 large mild onions, sliced
1 cup mushroom slices
2 tablespoons olive oil
2 cups cooked carrot slices
5 tomatoes, sliced

2 cups cooked Brussels sprouts
½ teaspoon thyme
¼ teaspoon salt
dash pepper
½ cup shredded Gruyère cheese
2 cups shredded mozzarella cheese

Preheat oven to 425 degrees F.

Sauté onions and mushrooms in olive oil. Drain and place on unbaked pizza crust. Place carrot slices, tomatoes, and Brussels sprouts on top. Sprinkle thyme, salt, and pepper over vegetables. Place Gruyère cheese and mozzarella cheese over top.

Bake at 425 degrees F for 15 to 20 minutes, until cheeses have melted and crust is golden brown.

Cut into 6 or 8 slices.

Pepper

Both black and white pepper come from berries that grow on the same woody vine.

When unripe berries are dried until they become dark greenish-black in color, they are called black pepper. White pepper is the ripened berries with the outer husks removed.

Pepper is one of the most popular spices in the world. When Columbus set sail for the Orient, the most important spice he was seeking was pepper. Its value was comparable to gold and, indeed, pepper was used to pay taxes, rents, and dowries.

Besides being added to foods as a seasoning, pepper has other uses. People in India drink water with pepper in it to stimulate their appetite, while in Holland and France pepper is sprinkled on carpets and furs when they are stored to repel moths.

About 25 tons of pepper are imported into the United States each year, most of it coming from Indonesia, India, Brazil, and Malaysia.

Pizza is enjoyed throughout the world with different toppings popular in different countries.

The favorite pizzas are:

Russia—sardines, tuna, mackerel, salmon, and onions
Mexico—shredded chicken and black bean sauce
Israel—feta cheese
Australia—eggs, bacon, onions, and tomatoes
France—cream
Chile—mussels and clams
England—tuna and corn
Japan—squid
Brazil—green peas
Bahamas—barbecued chicken and lots of spices
Guatemala—black bean sauce

Vegetable Pesto Pizza

Estelle Pirro
East Syracuse, New York

1 prepared 12-inch unbaked pizza crust
1 medium eggplant
salt
3 shallots, thinly sliced
1 tablespoon olive oil

1 cup Pesto Sauce (recipe follows)
2 cucumbers, peeled and sliced $\frac{1}{8}$-inch thick
1 cup ricotta cheese
1 cup shredded mozzarella cheese
$\frac{1}{2}$ cup alfalfa sprouts

Cut eggplant into thin slices, coat one side with salt, and let sit for 10 to 15 minutes. Turn over, coat other side with salt, and let sit another 10 to 15 minutes. Rinse well in cold water. Set aside.

Preheat oven to 425 degrees F.

Sauté shallots and eggplant slices in olive oil. Set aside.

Spoon Pesto Sauce on unbaked pizza crust. Spread shallots, eggplant slices, and cucumber slices over sauce. Sprinkle ricotta and mozzarella cheeses over top.

Bake at 425 degrees F for 12 to 15 minutes, until cheeses have melted and crust is golden brown.

Top with alfalfa sprouts.

Cut into 6 or 8 slices.

Pesto Sauce

1 garlic clove, sliced
½ cup olive oil
¼ cup freshly grated Parmesan or
Romano cheese
½ teaspoon salt

freshly ground pepper, to taste
3 tablespoons pine nuts
¼ cup chopped fresh parsley
2 cups fresh basil leaves, tightly
packed

Place garlic clove, olive oil, Parmesan or Romano cheese, salt, pepper, pine nuts, ⅛ cup of parsley, and 1 cup of basil leaves in a blender and blend until smooth. Add remaining ⅛ cup of parsley and remaining 1 cup of basil leaves and blend again until smooth.

Yield: 1 cup

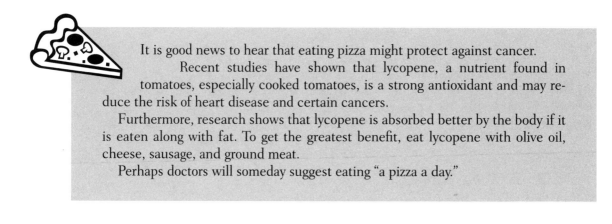

It is good news to hear that eating pizza might protect against cancer.

Recent studies have shown that lycopene, a nutrient found in tomatoes, especially cooked tomatoes, is a strong antioxidant and may reduce the risk of heart disease and certain cancers.

Furthermore, research shows that lycopene is absorbed better by the body if it is eaten along with fat. To get the greatest benefit, eat lycopene with olive oil, cheese, sausage, and ground meat.

Perhaps doctors will someday suggest eating "a pizza a day."

Vidalia Onion Pizza

Erica Copeland
Tacoma, Washington

1 prepared 12-inch unbaked pizza crust
2 cups thinly sliced Vidalia onions
¼ cup olive oil
1 cup minced Vidalia onions
2 garlic cloves, minced
1 cup sliced mushrooms
2 cups canned crushed tomatoes
1 6-ounce can tomato paste
1 teaspoon honey

3 bay leaves
1 teaspoon oregano
1 teaspoon parsley
1 teaspoon basil
½ teaspoon fennel seeds
¾ teaspoon salt
pepper to taste
1 cup shredded low-fat mozzarella cheese
½ cup grated Parmesan cheese

Sauté onion slices in olive oil in a large pan. Remove onions and set aside.

Sauté minced onions, garlic, and mushrooms in the same pan, until onions and mushrooms are soft. Add crushed tomatoes, tomato paste, honey, bay leaves, oregano, parsley, basil, fennel seeds, salt, and pepper. Bring to a boil, reduce heat to a simmer, and continue cooking, stirring often, until sauce thickens.

Preheat oven to 425 degrees F.

Remove thickened sauce from heat and take out the three bay leaves. Pour sauce onto unbaked pizza crust. Arrange onion slices on sauce. Sprinkle mozzarella cheese and Parmesan cheese over top.

Bake at 425 degrees F for 15 to 20 minutes, until cheeses have melted and crust is golden brown.

Cut into 6 or 8 slices.

Mushroom and Squash Pesto Pizza

Seth Toone
Murray, Utah

1 prepared 12-inch unbaked pizza crust
1 cup Pesto Sauce (recipe follows)
1½ cups sliced Portobello mushrooms

3 scallions, sliced
1½ cups sliced yellow squash
20 cherry tomatoes, cut into halves
2 cups shredded mozzarella cheese
½ cup grated Romano cheese

Preheat oven to 425 degrees F.

Prick unbaked pizza crust and bake at 425 degrees F for 10 minutes. Remove from oven and reduce oven to 350 degrees F.

Spoon Pesto Sauce on partially baked pizza crust. Spread mushrooms, scallions, and squash on sauce. Arrange cherry tomato halves around rim of pizza crust. Sprinkle mozzarella cheese and Romano cheese over top.

Bake at 350 degrees F for 15 to 20 minutes, until cheeses have melted and crust is golden brown.

Cut into 6 or 8 slices.

According to *Pizza Today* magazine, approximately 100 acres of pizza are consumed in the U.S. every 24 hours. That is 350 slices per second, 21,000 per minute, 1,260,000 per hour, and 30,240,000 slices every day.

Pesto Sauce

1 garlic clove, sliced
½ cup olive oil
¼ cup freshly grated Parmesan or
Romano cheese
½ teaspoon salt

freshly ground pepper, to taste
3 tablespoons pine nuts
¼ cup chopped fresh parsley
2 cups fresh basil leaves, tightly
packed

Place garlic clove, olive oil, Parmesan or Romano cheese, salt, pepper, pine nuts, ⅛ cup of parsley, and 1 cup of basil leaves in a blender and blend until smooth. Add remaining ⅛ cup of parsley and remaining 1 cup of basil leaves and blend again until smooth.

Yield: 1 cup

Garlic

Garlic is a member of the onion family and it is one of the oldest plants culti-vated by humans.

It was first grown in Central Asia and for a long time was considered as a food only for the lower classes. Besides being eaten as a food, garlic is also used as a medicine offering cures for and protection against diseases.

Another use for garlic was as a talisman, hung around the necks of children and livestock to repel evil spirits.

Red, Green, and Yellow Pepper Pizza

Patricia Nida
Dunbar, West Virginia

1 prepared 12-inch unbaked pizza
crust
2 red peppers, sliced
1 green pepper, sliced
1 yellow pepper, sliced
2 garlic cloves, crushed
1 cup chopped onions

3 tablespoons olive oil
2 tablespoons fresh parsley
1 teaspoon oregano
1 teaspoon basil
2 cups chopped tomatoes
1 teaspoon Worcestershire sauce
1 cup shredded Cheddar cheese

Preheat oven to 425 degrees F.

Sauté red peppers, green pepper, yellow pepper, garlic, and onions in olive oil. Add parsley, oregano, and basil. Stir in tomatoes and Worcestershire sauce. Simmer for about 5 minutes.

Spoon sauce onto unbaked pizza crust. Sprinkle Cheddar cheese over top.

Bake at 425 degrees F for 15 to 20 minutes, until cheese has melted and crust is golden brown.

Cut into 6 or 8 slices.

According to a report in the New York *Daily News*, Charo, the popular singer and dancer, favors lettuce-cucumber and salami-anchovy-pepperoni pizzas.

Pizza Primavera

Joanna Lara
Huntington Beach, California

1 prepared 12-inch unbaked pizza crust
1½ cups broccoli florettes
2 medium zucchini, sliced diagonally
1 pound young asparagus, ends removed and cut diagonally
1 cup fresh green peas

¼ cup olive oil
1 cup shredded mozzarella cheese
½ cup shredded Cheddar cheese
1 garlic clove, crushed
¼ teaspoon salt
dash pepper
1 cup sliced cherry tomatoes

Steam broccoli, zucchini, asparagus, and green peas until tender but crisp. Quickly transfer to a bowl of ice water to keep the bright colors. Let cool and then drain well.

Preheat oven to 400 degrees F.

Sprinkle 2 tablespoons of the olive oil over the unbaked pizza crust. Sprinkle mozzarella cheese, Cheddar cheese, garlic, salt, and pepper on crust. Arrange tomatoes, broccoli, zucchini, asparagus, and green peas over top.

Sprinkle remaining 2 tablespoons of olive oil over vegetables.

Bake at 400 degrees F for 15 to 20 minutes, until cheeses have melted and crust is golden brown.

Cut into 6 or 8 slices.

Pizza lovers take note: Post-it brand now offers its sticky notes in a new "flavor": one that smells like pizza.

Pizza Caprese

Primi Piatti Ristorante
Washington D.C.

Makes 8 servings

Pizza Dough (recipe follows)

Sprinkle flour on a working table. Proceed to take a ball of dough and flatten it out as thin as possible. You may want to use a wooden roller. Make tomato sauce out of plum tomatoes, garlic, fresh basil and a touch of oregano. Add salt and pepper to suit your own taste.

Spread the sauce on the dough, sprinkle with mozzarella cheese and bake inside a brick oven until it is crispy. Do not use too much cheese, just enough to give it a thin layer. You will have to check the pizza once to make sure it is not over or under done. Take it out and sprinkle with chopped basil.

Pizza Stracchino Cheese and Fresh Arugula

Primi Piatti Ristorante
Washington D.C.

Makes for 8 servings

Pizza Dough (recipe follows)

Sprinkle flour on a working table. Proceed to take a ball of dough and flatten it out as thin as possible. You may want to use a wooden roller.

Sprinkle a small amount of stracchino cheese on top and bake inside a brick oven until it is crispy. You will have to check the pizza once to make sure it is not over or under done. Take it out and sprinkle with chopped arugula.

Primi Piatti Ristorante Basic Dough

20 grams of yeast (dried active)
½ liter of water
30 grams of salt

approximately 100 cc of extra virgin olive oil
850 grams of flour 00 (brand 5 Stagioni preferably)

Mix yeast with water which is at room temperature (37 degrees C), until it is all dissolved. Add salt, olive oil, and flour. Work the dough with your hands for about 6-8 minutes until it becomes smooth and like an elastic ball of dough.

Leave the dough on the working table and cover it up with a damp cloth for about 10 minutes. When the 10 minutes are up, work the dough with your hands for another 10 minutes and then cover again with a damp cloth for an additional 10 minutes.

When the final 10 minutes are up, shape the dough in balls—each weighing about 165 grams. Sprinkle all the balls with flour in addition to the insides of a rectangular shaped plastic container.

Place all the balls inside the container and cover with a damp cloth. Then close the container with a secure lid and let dough rise for about $2\frac{1}{2}$ hours.

True pizza lovers have cause for celebration. In a recent article in the *New York Times,* food writer Eric Asimov gives the good news that classic New York pizza is back.

Classic New York pizza, Mr. Asimov writes, is pizza cooked quickly in extremely hot ovens, usually coal-fired, and has thin crusts with a charred, smoky crispness. The dough is prepared each day, real mozzarella cheese is used, the tomatoes are the best available, and the toppings are simple and added only in moderation. Furthermore, each pizza is cooked to order and never, ever sold by the slice.

Pizzas from the Sea

Shrimp Parmesan Pizza

Allan Lane
Fair Lawn, New Jersey

1 prepared 12-inch unbaked pizza crust
20 medium-sized shrimp
1 1-pound can plum tomatoes, mashed
3 garlic cloves, sliced

¼ teaspoon oregano
¼ teaspoon basil
1 tablespoon olive oil
1¼ cups shredded mozzarella cheese
½ cup grated Parmesan cheese

Boil shrimp until firm, drain, and then cut into small pieces. Set aside.

Preheat oven to 425 degrees F.

Heat plum tomatoes in a saucepan and add shrimp pieces. Simmer for 5 minutes. Stir in garlic, oregano, and basil. Set aside.

Spread olive oil on unbaked pizza crust. Pour tomato and shrimp sauce over crust. Sprinkle mozzarella and Parmesan cheeses over top.

Bake at 425 degrees F for 15 to 20 minutes, until cheeses have melted and crust is golden brown.

Cut into 6 or 8 slices.

Salmon and Feta Pizza

Cindy Worley
Mesa, Arizona

1 prepared 12-inch unbaked pizza crust
1 1-pound can crushed tomatoes
½ teaspoon oregano
1 teaspoon parsley
2 tablespoons capers

1 7½-ounce can salmon, drained, crumbled, with skin and bones removed
¾ cup crumbled feta cheese
1 cup shredded mozzarella cheese
3 hard boiled eggs, sliced

Preheat oven to 425 degrees F.

Spread crushed tomatoes on unbaked pizza crust. Sprinkle oregano and parsley over tomatoes. Place capers and salmon on top. Cover with feta and mozzarella cheeses.

Bake at 425 degrees F for 15 to 20 minutes, until cheeses have melted and crust is golden brown.

Decorate with slices of hard boiled eggs.

Cut into 6 or 8 slices.

 What do you do after you have been the head of the second most powerful nation on earth? For Mikhail S. Gorbachev, the former leader of the former Soviet Union, the answer was simple. He appeared in an advertisement for Pizza Hut, watching happily as his granddaughter devours a fresh slice.

Lox and Cream Cheese Pizza

Janice Vogel
Des Moines, Iowa

1 prepared 12-inch unbaked pizza crust
8 ounces low-fat cream cheese, softened

3 large tomatoes, sliced
2 red onions, sliced
6 ounces lox
3 tablespoons capers

Preheat oven to 425 degrees F.

Spread cream cheese on unbaked pizza crust. Bake at 425 degrees F for 15 to 20 minutes, until crust is golden brown.

Layer tomatoes, onions, and lox on baked crust. Scatter capers over top.

Cut into 6 or 8 slices.

For a little surprise, here is a listing of the three countries with the highest rate of pizza consumption.

In response to a question about what foods they had eaten within the last 24 hours, 16 percent of Americans and 18 percent of Italians said they had eaten pizza.

Pizza received its highest percentage in Argentina, where 20 percent of those interviewed said they had enjoyed a slice during that same time period.

Seafood Pizza

Theresa Jarrell
Wilmington, Delaware

1 prepared 12-inch unbaked pizza
crust
15 medium-sized shrimp
1 tablespoon olive oil
1 1-pound can chopped tomatoes
2 6½-ounce cans minced clams,
drained

1 small red pepper, chopped
1 small green pepper, chopped
2 garlic cloves, crushed
1 teaspoon parsley
salt, to taste
pepper, to taste
½ cup Parmesan cheese

Preheat oven to 425 degrees F.

Boil shrimp until firm, drain, and then cut into small pieces. Set aside.

Brush olive oil over unbaked pizza crust. Prick crust with fork.

Bake crust at 425 degrees F for approximately 15 minutes, until crust is golden brown.

Place shrimp, tomatoes, clams, red pepper, green pepper, garlic, parsley, salt, and pepper
in a saucepan and cook over low heat for approximately 15 minutes.

Spoon sauce over baked crust. Sprinkle Parmesan cheese over top.

Bake at 425 degrees F for 10 minutes more.

Cut into 6 or 8 slices.

Sardine and Egg Pizza

Jean Davenport
San Bernardino, California

1 prepared 12-inch unbaked pizza crust
1 10-ounce package frozen chopped kale, cooked and drained well
1 4¾-ounce can sardines in olive oil

1 cup crumbled feta cheese
1 cup shredded Cheddar cheese
4 hard-boiled eggs, sliced
1 teaspoon parsley

Preheat oven to 425 degrees F.

Spread kale on unbaked pizza crust. Add sardines, feta cheese, and Cheddar cheese.

Bake at 425 degrees F for 15 to 20 minutes, until cheeses have melted and crust is golden brown.

Arrange hard boiled egg slices around edge of pizza and then sprinkle parsley over egg slices.

Cut into 6 or 8 slices.

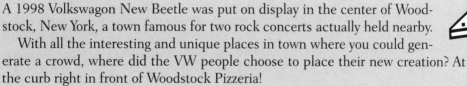

A 1998 Volkswagon New Beetle was put on display in the center of Woodstock, New York, a town famous for two rock concerts actually held nearby.

With all the interesting and unique places in town where you could generate a crowd, where did the VW people choose to place their new creation? At the curb right in front of Woodstock Pizzeria!

Surf and Turf Pizza

Dora Bennett
Anchorage, Alaska

1 prepared 12-inch unbaked pizza crust
2 teaspoons olive oil
8 anchovies, cut into thirds
½ cup thin pepperoni slices
2 cups sliced Portobello mushrooms

2 large Caramelized Onions (recipe follows)
1 garlic clove, crushed
½ cup tomato sauce
1 cup shredded Monterey Jack cheese
½ cup shredded mozzarella cheese

Preheat oven to 425 degrees F.

Spread olive oil on unbaked pizza crust. Place anchovies, pepperoni, mushrooms, onions, and garlic on crust. Cover with tomato sauce. Sprinkle Monterey Jack and mozzarella cheeses over top.

Bake at 425 degrees F for 15 to 20 minutes, until cheeses have melted and crust is golden brown.

Cut into 6 or 8 slices.

Caramelized Onions

¼ cup olive oil
2 large onions, sliced

salt
pepper

Heat the olive oil over medium heat in a large heavy pan. Add the onion slices, decrease heat to medium-low, cover, and cook with occasional stirring.

Continue cooking for about 25 to 30 minutes, until onions become soft and just begin to turn color. Remove cover. Sprinkle with salt and pepper.

Increase heat to medium and cook without the cover another 25 to 30 minutes with frequent stirring until onions are golden brown.

The Associazione Vera Pizza Napoletana—Association of True Neapolitan Pizza—a trade group in Naples, Italy, has set strict rules on what can be called a true Neapolitan pizza.

Such a pizza must have olive oil, buffalo mozzarella cheese, San Marzano tomatoes, special flour, handmade dough, and crust that is well done, somewhat soft and not crusty, has a high soft edge, and is not too thin. The pizza must also be baked in an oven made of brick or similar material and heated by wood.

Restaurants that meet the strict Neapolitan requirements are awarded a certificate of authenticity to be proudly displayed. The Neapolitan certification is not easily gained considering that by the end of 1997, less than 100 pizza restaurants around the world had won this stamp of approval.

If you think that designating exactly what is Neapolitan pizza is not a serious endeavor, consider this: Carlo Mangoni, a professor of nutrition, researched and wrote a 42-page treatise defining true Neapolitan pizza.

Seafood Marinara Pizza

Molly Burch
Houston, Texas

1 prepared 12-inch unbaked pizza crust
2 garlic cloves, minced
1 large green pepper, sliced
1½ tablespoons olive oil
1¼ cups prepared marinara sauce

2 to 4 tablespoons butter or margarine
2½ cups chopped cooked seafood, combination of your choice of shrimp, lobster, crab, clams, mussels, calamari

Preheat oven to 425 degrees F.

Sauté garlic and green pepper slices in olive oil in a large pan until pepper slices are soft. Add marinara sauce to pan, cover, and simmer for 20 minutes. Set aside.

Prick unbaked pizza crust and bake at 425 degrees F for 10 to 12 minutes. Remove crust from oven and reduce heat to 350 degrees F. Set aside.

Melt butter or margarine in a pan and add chopped cooked seafood and sauté for 4 to 5 minutes. Remove from pan and drain.

Add seafood to marinara sauce and spoon onto partially baked pizza crust.

Bake at 350 degrees F for 15 to 20 minutes, until crust is golden brown.

Cut into 6 or 8 slices.

There are more than 2,000 pizza restaurants in the Chicago area and, not surprisingly, Chicago has the highest annual per capita consumption of pizza of any place in the United States.

Prosciutto Seafood Pizza

Marie Ellen Collier
Bellevue, Washington

1 prepared 12-inch unbaked pizza crust
1¼ cups mushroom slices
2 garlic cloves minced
¼ cup olive oil
8 ounces prosciutto, thinly sliced
8 plum tomatoes, chopped

¾ cup chopped clams or mussels or a combination of the two
¼ teaspoon parsley
½ teaspoon oregano
1½ cups shredded mozzarella cheese
¼ cup grated Parmesan cheese

Preheat oven to 425 degrees F.

Sauté mushrooms and garlic in olive oil. Place on unbaked pizza crust. Add prosciutto, tomatoes, and clams or mussels. Sprinkle parsley, oregano, mozzarella cheese, and Parmesan cheese over top.

Bake at 425 degrees F for 15 to 20 minutes, until cheeses have melted and crust is golden brown.

Cut into 6 or 8 slices.

Olive Oil

There are strict standards for "virgin" olive oil. The oil must be gotten from the fruit of the olive tree in such a way that the conditions, especially the thermal conditions, do not cause any changes in the oil. In addition, the olives must not have been treated with anything but washing, centrifugation, and filtration.

There are several different grades of olive oil as defined by the International Olive Oil Council:

- Extra-Virgin Olive Oil has absolutely perfect taste and odor with an acidity of less than 1%.
- Fine Virgin Olive Oil has absolutely perfect taste and odor and a maximum acidity of less than 1.5%.
- Semi-fine Olive Oil—also called ordinary virgin olive oil—is virgin olive oil with good taste and odor and a maximum acidity of 3%.

Besides being so useful in cooking a wide variety of dishes, olive oil has been used for years as an ingredient in many folk remedies. Some of the ills cured by olive oil mixtures are dull hair, dandruff, dry skin, wrinkles, weak nails, tired feet, aching muscles, acne, hangovers, and high blood pressure.

Stan and Jan Berenstain are the authors of many enjoyable books for both children and adults.

One of their most delicious is "PAPA'S PIZZA: A Berenstain Bear Sniffy Book" with eight smells to scratch and sniff.

Join Papa Bear as he twirls the dough; cuts up tomatoes, onions, and mushrooms; adds the cheese; sprinkles some oregano; and puts the pizza in the oven. Scatch and sniff tomato, cheese, onion, mushrooms, oregano, smoke from the oven, and, finally, the baked pizza itself.

(Our copy of PAPA'S PIZZA is 20 years old and the scratch and sniff smells are still strong!)

Spicy Shrimp Pizza

Granita
Chef Jennifer Naylor
Malibu, California

Topping

3 cups grated mozzarella cheese
2 cups grated fontina cheese
1 pound plum tomatoes, ends
removed and sliced thin
4 teaspoons grated Parmesan cheese

1 pound Marinated Shrimp (recipe
follows)
1 medium red onion, sliced thinly
½ pound goat cheese

Marinated Shrimp

1 pound medium shrimp, peeled
and deveined
½ cup olive oil
3 tablespoons lemon juice

2 teaspoons chopped jalapeño
large pinch chopped cilantro
salt

Pizza Dough (recipe follows)

Prosciutto Pizza with Chino Tomatoes

Granita
Malibu, California

¾ pound prosciutto, thinly sliced and cut into ½-inch strips
½ pound yellow cherry tomatoes
½ pound red cherry tomatoes
3 tablespoons basil, thinly sliced
3 cups grated mozzarella cheese
2 cups grated fontina cheese

4 teaspoons grated Parmesan cheese
2 bunches baby arugula, stemmed and washed
1½ tablespoons balsamic vinegar
2½ tablespoons olive oil
salt
freshly ground black pepper

Pizza Dough (recipe follows)

Granita Pizza Dough

Makes 4 7- or 8-inch pizza crusts

1 package active dry or fresh yeast
1 teaspoon honey or sugar
¾ cup warm water

2¾ cups all-purpose flour
1 teaspoon salt
2 tablespoons olive oil, plus additional for brushing

In a small bowl, dissolve the yeast and honey in ¼ cup of the warm water.

In a mixer fitted with a dough hook, combine the flour and the salt. Pour in 2 tablespoons of the oil and when absorbed, scrape in the dissolved yeast. Add the remaining ½ cup water and knead on low speed about 5 minutes.

Turn out onto a board and knead 2 or 3 minutes longer. Dough should be smooth and firm. Let rise in a warm spot, covered with a damp towel, about 30 minutes. (Dough will stretch when lightly pulled.)

Divide the dough into 4 balls, about 6 ounces each. Work each ball by pulling down the sides and tucking under the bottom of the ball. Repeat 4 or 5 times. Then on a smooth unfloured surface, roll the ball under the palm of your hand until the dough is smooth and firm, about 1 minute. Cover with a damp towel and let rest 15 to 20 minutes. At this point, the balls can be loosely covered with plastic wrap and refrigerated for 1 to 2 days.

Preheat oven to 525 degrees F. Place a pizza stone in the oven.

To prepare each pizza, place a ball of dough on a lightly floured surface. Press down on the center, spreading the dough, or roll into a 7-inch or 8-inch circle, with the outer border a little thicker than the inner circle. Brush lightly with oil and arrange the toppings of your choice only over the inner circle.

Arrange the pizza on the baking stone and bake 15 to 20 minutes, or until the pizzas are nicely browned. Transfer to a firm surface and cut into slices with a pizza cutter. Serve immediately.

In her first important role, Julia Roberts played a young woman working in a pizza parlor in the movie "Mystic Pizza," set in the real life seaside resort town of Mystic, Connecticut. What better way to start on the road to stardom in Hollywood than with a good pizza?

Smoked Salmon Pizza with Dill Creme Fraiche and Caviar

Chefs Mitchell and Steven Rosenthal
Postrio
San Francisco, California

Pizza Dough (recipe follows)

4 tablespoons extra virgin olive oil
½ red onion, sliced very thinly
Dill Creme Fraiche (recipe follows)
3–4 ounces smoked salmon, sliced thinly (3 slices per pizza)

4 tablespoons caviar (golden or black)
2 teaspoons fresh chives

Preheat the oven to 500 degrees F.

Lightly flour a work surface. Roll or stretch Pizza Dough into 4 8-inch circles.

Place the pizzas on a lightly floured wooden peel. Brush the centers of the circles to within 1 inch of the edge with olive oil. Sprinkle the red onion slices lightly on the dough.

Slide the pizza crusts onto the stone and bake 8–10 minutes. When they are golden brown, transfer them from the oven to a bread board.

Spread the Dill Creme Fraiche evenly over the pizza dough and arrange the sliced salmon over the dough. Cut the pizzas into 8 slices and place a spoonful of caviar into the center of each pizza. Sprinkle the pizzas with the chives.

Dill Creme Fraiche

½ cup crème fraiche (you can substitute sour cream)
½ cup sour cream

2 tablespoons chopped fresh dill
2 shallots, chopped fine

In a small bowl whisk together the crème fraiche, sour cream, dill and shallots; season with salt and pepper.

Pizza Dough

Makes enough dough for 4 small pizzas

1 teaspoon salt
1 tablespoon honey
2 tablespoons olive oil
¾ cup cold water

1 package fresh or dry yeast
¼ cup warm water
3 cups all purpose flour

In a small bowl combine the salt, honey, olive oil and ¾ cup of cold water.

Dissolve the yeast in the ¼ cup of warm water and let proof for 10 minutes. Place the flour in a food processor, with motor running, slowly pour the salt and honey liquid through the feed tube. Then pour in the dissolved yeast. Process until dough forms a ball on the blade. If it is sticky, add sprinklings of flour.

Transfer the dough to a lightly floured surface and knead until it is smooth. Place in a buttered bowl and allow the dough to rest for 30 minutes. Divide the dough into 4 equal parts. Roll each piece into a smooth, tight ball. Place on a flat sheet or dish and cover with a damp towel and refrigerate.

One hour before baking, remove the dough from the refrigerator and let it come to room temperature.

Global Pizzas

Refried Bean and Beef Pizza

Pamela Andrade
Warwick, Rhode Island

1 prepared 12-inch unbaked pizza crust
1 cup sour cream
2 cups refried beans
2 cups shredded cooked beef
2 cups crumbled tortilla chips

¾ cup taco sauce
3 green onions, chopped
½ cup chopped black olives
1 teaspoon chili powder
hot pepper sauce, to taste
1 cup shredded Cheddar cheese

Preheat oven to 425 degrees F.

Spread sour cream, beans, beef, tortilla chips, taco sauce, onions, black olives, chili powder, and hot pepper sauce on unbaked pizza crust. Sprinkle Cheddar cheese over top.

Bake at 425 degrees F for 15 to 20 minutes, until cheese has melted and crust is golden brown.

Cut into 6 or 8 slices.

Chicken Chimichanga Pizza

Gloria Wiggins
Cayce, South Carolina

1 prepared 12-inch unbaked pizza crust
2 scallions, chopped
2 tablespoons olive oil
2 to 3 green chili peppers, thinly sliced

1 green bell pepper, seeded and thinly sliced
3 cups shredded cooked chicken
½ cup black olives, chopped
¾ cup grated Cheddar cheese
½ cup shredded Monterey Jack cheese

Preheat oven to 425 degrees F.

Sauté scallions in olive oil until soft. Add chili peppers and green bell pepper and sauté for 3 to 5 minutes more.

Remove from heat and add chicken.

Spread on unbaked pizza crust. Sprinkle black olives, cheddar cheese, and Monterey Jack cheese over top.

Bake at 425 degrees F for 15 to 20 minutes, until cheeses have melted and crust is golden brown.

Cut into 6 or 8 slices.

Considering that Ted Turner, the television mogul, and his wife Jane Fonda raise bison on their ranch in Montana, it should not be a big surprise that bison pizza is Mr. Turner's favorite.

Mid-Eastern Pizza

Betty Szewczak
Chester, Pennsylvania

1 prepared 12-inch unbaked pizza crust
1¼ pound ground lamb
1 cup chopped onions
¼ cup olive oil
¼ cup tomato paste
1 cup water

¼ cup raisins
1½ teaspoons ground cumin
½ teaspoon ground cloves
¼ pound prepared hummus
½ cup sliced green olives with pimentos
¼ cup chopped pistachio nuts

Preheat oven to 425 degrees F.

Place lamb, onions, and olive oil in a pan and cook until browned. Drain and return to pan. Add tomato paste, water, raisins, cumin, and cloves. Simmer until most of the liquid is gone. Stir in hummus, olives, and pistachio nuts.

Spread on unbaked pizza crust and bake at 425 degrees F for 15 to 20 minutes until crust is golden brown.

Cut into 6 or 8 slices.

The Hansons might be world famous singing stars now, but it was not too long ago that the three brothers were singing a cappella for fun in pizza parlors back in their hometown of Tulsa, Oklahoma.

Spaghetti Sauce Pizza

Laura Hinton
Midfield, Alabama

1 prepared 12-inch unbaked pizza crust
1 1-pound jar of meat-flavored spaghetti sauce
½ cup thin pepperoni slices

8 sun-dried tomatoes, chopped
2 cups sliced mushrooms
1 large mild onion, thinly sliced
¾ cup shredded Cheddar cheese
1 cup shredded mozzarella cheese

Preheat oven to 425 degrees F.

Spread spaghetti sauce on unbaked pizza crust. Place pepperoni, sun-dried tomatoes, mushrooms, and onion slices on spaghetti sauce. Sprinkle Cheddar and mozzarella cheeses over top.

Bake at 425 degrees F for 15 to 20 minutes, until cheeses have melted and crust is golden brown.

Cut into 6 or 8 slices.

After 128 days in space on the Russian space station Mir, what food did American Astronaut Dr. David Wolf miss most? Pepperoni and mushroom pizza! At his request, just such a pizza was waiting for Dr. Wolf when the space shuttle Endeavor recently touched down at Kennedy Space Center in Florida.

Prosciutto and Broccoli Pizza

Rosemarie Kimbrough
Highland Park, Michigan

1 prepared 12-inch unbaked pizza crust
2 cups chopped broccoli florettes
¼ cup olive oil
1 red bell pepper, seeded and cut into thin strips
1 cup chopped onions
1 garlic clove, minced
1½ cup pizza sauce
6 ounces prosciutto, cut into strips
1½ cups shredded mozzarella cheese
6 ounces Provolone cheese, thinly sliced in strips

Preheat oven to 425 degrees F.

Boil broccoli in water until tender but crisp. Drain and set aside.

Heat olive oil in a large pan, add pepper and onions, and sauté until soft. Add garlic and sauté for 1 to 2 minutes. Remove from heat. Stir in pizza sauce and spread on unbaked pizza crust.

Arrange broccoli and prosciutto over top. Sprinkle mozzarella cheese and Provolone cheese on pizza.

Bake at 425 degrees F for 15 to 20 minutes, until cheeses have melted and crust is golden brown.

Cut into 6 or 8 slices.

Seen on a sweatshirt in a clothing store window on Main Street in Annapolis, Maryland, around Thanksgiving: an embroidered turkey holding up a sign saying "Order Pizza."

Canadian Bacon and Vegetable Pizza

Melissa Austin
Louisville, Kentucky

1 prepared 12-inch unbaked pizza crust
1 1-pound can crushed tomatoes
1 tablespoon olive oil
2 garlic cloves, crushed
½ pound Canadian bacon, cooked and cut into pieces

1 green pepper, chopped
1 cup sliced mushrooms
½ cup sliced black olives
1 cup chopped broccoli
2 cups shredded mozzarella cheese

Preheat oven to 425 degrees F.

Spread crushed tomatoes on unbaked pizza crust. Sprinkle olive oil and crushed garlic over top. Place Canadian bacon, green pepper, mushroom slices, olive slices, and broccoli on crust. Cover with mozzarella.

Bake at 425 degrees F for 15 to 20 minutes, until cheese has melted and crust is golden brown.

Cut into 6 or 8 slices.

According to the National Restaurant Association, pizza is the second most served food in restaurants in the United States, out-ranked only by hamburgers.

Greek Pizza

Julia Betzen
Haysville, Kansas

1 prepared 12-inch unbaked pizza crust
1 pound ground lamb, cooked and drained
2 cups sliced squash or zucchini

¾ cup Greek olives, pitted
1 cup cherry tomato slices
½ cup crumbled feta cheese
1 cup shredded mozzarella cheese

Preheat oven to 425 degrees F.

Spread cooked lamb, squash or zucchini, Greek olives, and tomatoes on unbaked pizza crust. Sprinkle feta cheese on top and cover with mozzarella cheese.

Bake at 425 degrees F for 15 to 20 minutes, until cheeses have melted and crust is golden brown.

Cut into 6 or 8 slices.

It seems there is no limit to the variety of pizzas Americans love. One recent example is Dairy Queen's DQ TREATZZA PIZZA. Think of cake and fudge crunch formed into a round crust, a layer of vanilla or chocolate ice cream instead of tomato sauce, and toppings of M&M's, peanut butter fudge, Heath bar candy pieces, and a choice of fruit sauces including strawberry/banana, raspberry, and blackberry.

It's a long way from sausage and oregano, but an appealing alternative on those too-hot-to-bake days of summer!

Mexican Pizza

Ben Lacour
Gretna, Louisiana

1 prepared 12-inch unbaked pizza crust
1 cup salsa
1 tablespoon crushed red chili pepper
dash hot sauce

1 15-ounce can refried beans
1 cup cooked ground beef
1 cup chopped onions
¼ cup chopped fresh cilantro
1 cup shredded Cheddar cheese
1 cup shredded mozzarella

Preheat oven to 425 degrees F.

Mix together salsa, red chili pepper, and hot sauce and spread on unbaked pizza crust. Cover with refried beans, cooked ground beef, chopped onions, and cilantro. Sprinkle Cheddar cheese and mozzarella cheese over top.

Bake at 425 degrees F for 15 to 20 minutes, until cheeses have melted and crust is golden brown.

Cut into 6 or 8 slices.

Cilantro

Cilantro is the Spanish name for the leaves of the plant whose seeds are known as coriander.

Cilantro is also called Chinese parsley and has a taste like a blend of lemon and parsley. It is very popular in Mexican and Asian cooking.

Lamb Pizza

Chef Premnah Motiram
Bombay Palace
New York, New York

Prepare a 6-inch naan (Indian bread) and then bake in a tandoori clay oven until puffy.

Cook a lamb kabab on a skewer and then slice the meat into bite-sized pieces. Cook the meat with sautéed onion, and red and green peppers. Season the sauté with coriander and curry leaf.

Spread mixture on the naan and then sprinkle with shredded cow's milk cheese.

The pizza is finished by placing in the broiler.

Appetizer and Dessert Pizzas

Goat Cheese and Garlic Pizza

Angie Whitehead
Richmond, Virginia

1 prepared 12-inch unbaked pizza crust
½ cup olive oil
1 28-ounce can crushed tomatoes
6 to 8 garlic cloves, chopped

1 teaspoon oregano
1 cup crumbled goat cheese
½ cup shredded Gruyère
1 tablespoon chopped fresh basil leaves

Preheat oven to 425 degrees F.

Brush unbaked pizza crust with ¼ cup olive oil. Place tomatoes and garlic on crust. Sprinkle oregano, goat cheese, and Gruyère cheese on top. Drizzle remaining ¼ cup olive oil over cheeses.

Bake at 425 degrees F for 15 to 20 minutes, until cheeses have melted and crust is golden brown.

Sprinkle basil leaves over top.

Cut into 6 or 8 slices.

Sun-Dried Tomato and Garlic Pizza

Bessie Huddleston
Garland, Texas

1 prepared 12-inch unbaked pizza crust
¾ cup sun dried tomatoes
4 garlic cloves, minced
1 teaspoon basil

½ teaspoon thyme
1 cup nonfat ricotta cheese
1 cup shredded nonfat mozzarella cheese

Preheat oven to 425 degrees F.

Soak sun-dried tomatoes in hot water for 15 minutes, until desired softness. Drain. Arrange tomatoes on unbaked pizza crust. Cover with garlic, basil, thyme, ricotta cheese, and mozzarella cheese.

Bake at 425 degrees F for 15 to 20 minutes, until cheeses have melted and crust is golden brown.

Cut into 6 or 8 slices.

Basil

Basil, a member of the mint family, gets its aroma and flavor from the essential oils of the plant.

It is used not only to flavor a variety of dishes but also to season one's life. Hindus plant basil around their homes and temples to ensure happiness while young Italians traditionally wear basil to show that they are in love.

Basil is grown in the United States as well as France and Hungary.

Hawaiian Pizza

Clara Ackerman
Evanston, Illinois

1 prepared 12-inch unbaked pizza crust
8 pineapple rings, drained well
6 ounces ham, sliced or cut into cubes
1 10-ounce package frozen spinach, cooked and drained well
1 cup ricotta cheese
dash ground cloves
¼ cup grated Parmesan cheese

Preheat oven to 400 degrees F.

Spread pineapple rings, ham, spinach, and ricotta cheese on unbaked pizza crust. Sprinkle cloves and Parmesan cheese over top.

Bake at 400 degrees F for 13 to 17 minutes, until cheeses have melted and crust is golden brown.

Cut into 6 or 8 slices.

On a per capita basis, Des Moines, Iowa, is the number one city in the United States for eating frozen pizza. People there eat two-and-one-half times as much frozen pizza as the rest of the country and four times as much as people in Los Angeles.

Des Moines is followed by Minneapolis/St. Paul, Minnesota, second, and then, in turn, by St. Louis, Missouri; Omaha, Nebraska; Denver, Colorado; Charlotte, North Carolina; Indianapolis, Indiana; Chicago, Illinois; and Memphis, Tennessee.

Avocado and Brie Pizza

Tina Plummer
Washington DC

1 prepared 12-inch unbaked pizza crust
1 large mild onion, thinly sliced
¼ cup fresh parsley
8 ounces Brie cheese, thinly sliced

1 cup ricotta cheese
3 tablespoons chopped walnuts
2 large avocados, peeled, pitted, and sliced
¼ cup grated Parmesan cheese

Preheat oven to 375 degrees F.

Place onion slices on unbaked pizza crust. Sprinkle parsley over onion slices. Evenly spread Brie cheese slices on top. Spread ricotta cheese and then sprinkle walnuts over ricotta cheese.

Bake at 375 degrees F for 15 to 20 minutes, until cheeses have melted and crust is golden brown.

Remove from oven and arrange avocado slices on top. Sprinkle with Parmesan cheese.

Return to oven and bake for 5 minutes more.

Cut into 6 or 8 slices.

Talk about home-delivery of your pizza and Lou Malnati's PIZZERIA of Northbrook, Illinois, comes to mind.

They offer a mail-order deep-dish pizza with a choice of cheese, pepperoni, and sausage toppings that serves two or three.

The pizza comes partially baked. You do the rest of the job yourself.

Pineapple and Kiwi Pizza

Lucy Blankenship
Beech Grove, Indiana

1 prepared 12-inch unbaked pizza crust
1 cup whole berry cranberry sauce
1 cup cottage cheese

1 20-ounce can crushed pineapple in own juice, drained
4 kiwi fruits, peeled and sliced
fresh mint leaves

Preheat oven to 425 degrees F.

Spread cranberry sauce over unbaked pizza crust. Bake at 425 degrees F for 15 to 20 minutes, until crust is golden brown.

Spread cottage cheese, pineapple, and kiwi fruit slices over cranberry sauce. Decorate with mint leaves.

Chill in refrigerator.

Cut into 6 or 8 slices.

One major airline encourages its agents at the airport to offer "creative amenities" to passengers whose flights are delayed more than two hours. For example, they will order pizza from a favorite non-airport restaurant to be delivered to waiting passengers stuck at the terminal. (Now, if only they could do something about the food served on the plane. . . .)

Avocado and Pecan Pizza

Nathan Rhodes
Towson, Maryland

1 prepared 12-inch unbaked pizza crust
½ cup nonfat plain yogurt
1 cup asparagus tips
2 Caramelized Onions (recipe follows)

¾ cup chopped pecans
½ cup crumbled blue cheese
½ cup shredded mozzarella cheese
2 avocados, peeled, pitted, and sliced
watercress sprigs

Preheat oven to 425 degrees F.

Coat unbaked pizza crust with yogurt. Place asparagus, onions, pecans, blue cheese, and mozzarella cheese over yogurt.

Bake at 425 degrees F for 15 minutes.

Remove from oven and arrange avocado slices on top.

Return to oven and bake 5 minutes more.

Remove from oven and garnish with watercress sprigs.

Cut into 6 or 8 slices.

Caramelized Onions

½ cup olive oil
2 large onions, sliced

salt
pepper

Heat the olive oil over medium heat in a large heavy pan. Add the onion slices, decrease heat to medium-low, cover, and cook with occasional stirring.

Continue cooking for about 25 to 30 minutes, until onions become soft and just begin to turn color. Remove cover. Sprinkle with salt and pepper.

Increase heat to medium and cook without the cover another 25 to 30 minutes with frequent stirring until onions are golden brown.

Have you always dreamed of baking traditional wood-fired pizza in an authentic clay oven made in Tuscany, Italy?

Your dream can come true with just such an oven being offered by Hammacher Schlemmer, the purveyor of innovative products with a mail order catalog; stores in New York City, Chicago, and Beverly Hills.

The oven can be yours for just $18,000. And that price not only includes delivery and set up, but you also get a mailing every three months with seasonal recipes and cooking techniques.

(We think your regular oven makes a pretty good pizza as well!)

Blue Cheese and Pear Pizza

Rosalind Anthony
Garner, North Carolina

1 prepared 12-inch unbaked pizza crust
½ cup apricot jam
½ cup crumbled blue cheese
4 pears, cored and sliced

1 cup dried cranberries
¼ teaspoon cinnamon mixed with 2 teaspoons sugar
½ cup low-fat yogurt with fruit

Preheat oven to 425 degrees F.

Prick unbaked pizza crust and spread with apricot jam.

Bake at 425 degrees F for 15 minutes. Remove from oven and reduce heat to 325 degrees F.

Put blue cheese, pears, and cranberries on crust. Sprinkle cinnamon sugar over top.

Bake at 325 degrees F for 10 minutes. Remove from oven and spoon yogurt over top.

Cut into 6 or 8 slices.

"Trufflemania," as the craze for both black and white versions of the expensive fungi is being called, has brought us truffle butter, truffle juice, truffle cheese, and truffle pasta.

Not to be left out, pizza is also part of "Trufflemania." Some restaurants are drizzling white truffle oil on pizza.

Chocolate Pizza

Timothy Gilchrist
Parma, Ohio

1 prepared 12-inch unbaked pizza crust
1 pound semisweet chocolate, melted
1 cup mini-marshmallows
½ cup vanilla chips
½ cup chopped maraschino cherries
½ cup peanut butter chips
½ cup chopped walnuts, pecans, or hazelnuts
½ cup canned plums, drained and chopped
2 kiwi fruits, peeled and sliced
½ cup drained mandarin oranges
1 cup flaked coconut

Preheat oven to 375 degrees F.

Bake crust at 375 degrees F for 15 to 20 minutes, until crust is golden brown.

Remove from oven, let crust cool, and then spread melted chocolate onto crust. Using a dull knife, draw 8 equal slices in the chocolate.

Fill one slice with mini-marshmallows, one slice with vanilla chips, one slice with maraschino cherries, one slice with peanut butter chips, one slice with nuts, one slice with plums, one slice with kiwi fruit, and one slice with mandarin oranges.

Sprinkle coconut over entire pizza.

Cut into 16 slices.

Salads on the Side

Two-Cheese Garden Salad

1 head red leaf lettuce, rinsed, drained, and torn into small pieces
1 cup kolrabi pieces, rinsed and drained
½ cup radicchio pieces, rinsed and drained
½ cup chopped walnuts
½ cup sliced green olives with pimentos

½ cup grated Cheddar cheese
½ cup crumbled feta cheese
½ cup sliced mushrooms
6 to 8 radishes, sliced
1 large red or yellow bell pepper, seeded and diced
1 cup fresh peas

In a large salad bowl toss red leaf lettuce, kolrabi, radicchio, walnuts, green olives, Cheddar cheese, feta cheese, mushrooms, radishes, red or yellow bell pepper, and peas.

Yield: 6 to 8 servings

Bacon and Egg Salad

1 head Boston lettuce, rinsed, drained, and torn into small pieces
1 cup mesclun or spring mix
4 large spinach leaves, rinsed, drained, and chopped
½ cup roasted and salted sunflower seeds
3 hard-boiled eggs, chopped

½ cup crisp bacon pieces
1 small mild onion, thinly sliced
½ cup crumbled blue cheese or Gorgonzola cheese
1 large green bell pepper, seeded and sliced
1 cup croutons

In a large salad bowl, toss Boston lettuce, mesclun or spring mix, spinach leaves, sunflower seeds, hard-boiled eggs, bacon, onion slices, and blue or Gorgonzola cheese.

Arrange pepper slices on top of salad and then sprinkle with croutons.

Yield: 6 to 8 servings

No matter where you go, it seems, you can always get pizza.

Tiny Easter Island in the Pacific is 1,400 miles from Pitcairn Island, the nearest inhabited land, and 2,340 miles from Chile which has owned Easter Island since 1888. But visitors who make the journey to this remote place to stand in awe before the famous and mysterious human-like statues do not have to rough it completely.

In Hanga Roa, the only town on Easter Island, there are several small hotels, curio shops, a disco, and, to ensure that civilization is not left too far behind, a pizza parlor.

Cranberry-Pecan Salad

½ head red-leaf lettuce, rinsed,
drained, and torn into small pieces
½ head iceberg lettuce, rinsed,
drained, and torn into small pieces
½ cup dried cranberries

½ cup chopped pecans
½ cup chopped black olives
½ cup sliced mushrooms
2 tablespoons chopped scallions
1 Belgium endive, chopped

In a large salad bowl, toss red-leaf lettuce, iceberg lettuce, cranberries, pecans, black olives, mushrooms, scallions, and Belgium endive.

Yield: 6 to 8 servings

During the 1996 Presidential campaign there was a clear choice of whom to vote for . . . and what to eat.

The forces for Bob Dole got food from restaurants and catering services and the Bill Clinton campaign went to supermarkets. The Natural Law Party, running on a platform based on the teachings of the Maharishi Mahesh Yogi, the guru who was a spiritual guide to the Beatles, not surprisingly ordered food from Thai and Indian restaurants.

And for billionaire Ross Perot's group—the Reform Party—it was usually pizza.

Marinated Mushrooms

½ cup water
⅔ cup olive oil
juice of 2 lemons
1 bay leaf

2 garlic cloves, crushed
6 whole peppercorns
¼ teaspoon salt
1 pound fresh small mushrooms,
brushed and trimmed

Combine water, olive oil, lemon juice, bay leaf, garlic, peppercorns, and salt in a saucepan. Heat to boiling, reduce heat, cover, and then simmer for 15 minutes. Remove bay leaf and peppercorns by straining and return liquid to pan. Add mushrooms, and simmer for 5 minutes, stirring constantly.

Remove from heat, let cool, and chill in refrigerator in covered container for 8 hours or overnight.

For serving, remove mushrooms from liquid with a slotted spoon.

Yield: 6 to 8 servings

It seems like Barbie does everything, goes everywhere, and always has just the right outfit.

It should be no surprise then that Barbie has a Cooking Magic Pizza Party with two pizzas, a pizza cutter, a pizza sauce container, a spatula, a bottle of soda, two cups, and two plates for serving the pizza.

The pizza changes color as you dip the spatula in ice water and spread it over the pizza. As the color changes, you see red sauce appear.

Tomato and Cucumber Salad

2 cups diced tomatoes
3 cups thinly sliced peeled
cucumbers
1 large mild onion, thinly sliced

3 tablespoons wine vinegar
2 teaspoons sugar
2 tablespoons chopped fresh basil
¼ cup olive oil

In a large-sized bowl, combine the tomatoes, cucumbers, onion slices, vinegar, sugar, basil, and olive oil.

Marinate in refrigerator for 8 hours or overnight.

Yield: 6 to 8 servings

The catalog from Chadwick's of Boston has just the thing for the first-time home pizza maker. The Deep-Dish Pizza Kit has everything you need to get started: a round pizza stone, crust mix, Italian spices, a pizza cutter, and instructions, all packed in an attractive 11½-inch dish for just $20.00. All you have to add are the toppings of your choice.

Cottage Cheese and Carrot Salad

1½ cups cottage cheese
1 cup Mandarin orange slices, drained
1 cup shredded carrots

½ cup raisins
½ cup sliced almonds
fresh spinach leaves, rinsed and patted dry

In a medium-sized bowl gently mix together cottage cheese, Mandarin orange slices, carrots, raisins, and almonds. Set aside.

Cover the bottom and sides of a shallow serving dish with the spinach leaves.

Evenly spread the cottage cheese mixture onto the spinach leaves.

Yield: 4 to 6 servings

They say that location is everything in real estate but for John Pashalis, who was looking for a place to open his new restaurant called Angelo's Pizza, he found something even more important than location.

He found a building in midtown Manhattan that had chimneys that were once used for burning coal to provide heat. Those chimneys allowed Mr. Pashalis to install the coal-fired brick ovens that give the traditional and highly desirable light char to thin-crusted pizzas.

INDEX